Elizabethan Stitches

A Guide to Historic English Needlework

by
Jacqui Carey

Acknowledgements

Although only one name is credited on the cover of this book, its existence would not have been possible without the efforts of many, too many to acknowledge here in full. As usual, book production has been a family affair with everyone adding vital ingredients, including cups of tea, corrections and encouragement. In addition, special mention should be made to Steve Pretty for working his way through the instructions, and providing insightful and wide-ranging comments. Thanks also to Lars and Beth Lea, for without their encouragement this book would have remained unwritten .

This book is based on research work that has been supported by a large network, from authors who make information accessible, to teachers and colleagues who willingly share their expertise. The study of surviving artefacts has been made possible thanks to numerous people, from receptionists to curators and collectors. Each has generously given their knowledge and kindness. The following groups and individuals deserve particular mention as having made a significant contribution to this particular project: Ashmolean Museum, Bodleian Library, British Library, Sir Richard and Lady Mary Carew Pole, Annette Collinge, Lord Daventry, Dorset County Museum, Embroiderers' Guild, Joy and Stephen Jarrett, Platt Hall Gallery of Costume, Salisbury and South Wiltshire Museum, Heather Toomer, Victoria & Albert Museum. Perhaps it is fitting that the 'last but not least' is reserved for the countless anonymous embroiderers, both now and then, who create something that is a joy to behold.

Front Cover: Embroidered panel
featured in Case Study 21 (page 140).
© *Embroiderers' Guild*

Published by Carey Company, Ottery St Mary, Devon, UK

ISBN 978-0 -9523225 -8 -0

Contents

Introduction

Old English textiles dating from the 16th to 17th century are fascinating objects. Surviving examples are visually intriguing and thought provoking, but unfortunately they have not endured in large quantities. An understanding of these textiles can be gained from documents and images dating from the period, but object-based research can offer insights not available from documented sources.

Historic English textiles can be viewed in museums, but close-up and detailed study of surviving objects is a privileged experience. The age and delicacy of the items usually means that access is restricted to help preserve the textiles. However, publications and close-up photography enables the research experience to be shared with a wider audience. In 2009, Jacqui Carey published *Sweet Bags: an Investigation into 16th and 17th Century Needlework* detailing some of her academic and practical research that centred on these particular textiles. *Elizabethan Stitches* has been produced in an effort to expand on the practical issues raised by the author's observations, and to aid those wishing to identify and reproduce historic items.

The author's detailed study of surviving artefacts has revealed that many of the stitches found on late sixteenth to early seventeenth century textiles differ from those used today. For over one hundred years, publications discussing historic English needlework have described the historic stitches in relation to the stitches made popular by women such as Thérèse de Dillmont, Grace Christie (writing as Mrs. Archibald Christie), and Mary Thomas. However, the visual evidence found on the surviving textiles does not correspond with these modern interpretations.

The structure of a stitch can be identified with certainty, and its physical form can be illustrated to show how it differs from other stitches. All the stitch structures shown in this book have been found on actual surviving items and are unequivocal. A modern stitch might produce a visually similar appearance, but is usually found to be a different structure to those seen on the original items. This in turn means that the techniques used to create the historic stitches must have differed from modern methods.

Although it is possible to recreate an exact copy of a historic stitch structure, there is no way of knowing the precise technique use to produce the original. Being able to reproduce a stitch is not definitive proof that the original was made in the same way. Indeed, it is almost impossible to accurately determine a technique from a finished structure. This is because there are many ways of achieving the same effect, with different techniques creating identical results. Sometimes additional evidence, or telltale characteristics can increase the likelihood of one particular technique being used rather than others, but there normally remains an element of doubt. Even if a method is well documented, further uncertainties exist about the precise way in which it has been constructed. This is because handiwork usually involves an element of an individual's manner, and can be rendered in a personal way. Therefore the techniques illustrated in this book are given as the option that seems the most plausible, though they are open to individual interpretation. Nonetheless, the authenticity of the stitch structure remains, and is illustrated with specific examples in the hope of re-establishing an understanding of the exquisite textiles that form part of our heritage.

Fig. 1. A borage motif from Case Study 22 (page 144).
© Witney Antiques.

Needlework

The needlework described in this book is not intended to cover all forms of stitching undertaken during the period extending around the Elizabethan era. Many different stitches were found on surviving objects, and this book will focus on some of those that have been misinterpreted in modern literature. It is worth pointing out that the needlework was found predominantly on high quality items thought to have belonged to the upper classes. During this era, textiles were expensive items, and one would reasonably associate the decorative 'fancy work' to be the prerogative of those with wealth and status. Objects of exceptional quality are more likely to be looked after better than the ordinary, everyday ones. This results in a bias in antiques, as top-end goods have a better rate of survival. Without more comprehensive evidence, it is difficult to assess the full extent of this style of work, and whether examples, made from more humble materials, existed lower down the social scale.

Terminology

Terminology can be used in various ways by different people and across different periods of time. This can cause confusion unless a specific definition is supplied to give meaning to the terms used in the circumstances. John Taylor's famous poem *The Praise of the Needle* and the list in Randle Holme's book provide us with a range of stitch names from the past, but unfortunately they cannot be accurately attributed to actual stitches. Although some of the names have survived into the present day, it is not possible to know if they refer to the same stitches being described in these two historic sources.

Today's terms can still be ambiguous. For instance, some stitches have several names, or more confusingly, one name can be attributed to several stitches. In keeping with popular opinion, this book uses modern stitch names as defined by Grace Christie and Mary Thomas, as they are frequently quoted as being the source of stitch terms, and many modern stitch dictionaries appear to stem from the work of these two authors.

Unfortunately, most of the stitches shown in this book have been obsolete for so long that they do not appear in stitch dictionaries. As a consequence, their original names have been lost. This presents a dilemma when one wishes to distinguish between each example. It has been decided to use the prefix of *Elizabethan* to identify names that have no established reference. This term was selected as the earliest textiles detailed in this book date from the Elizabethan era. In order to help explain precise detail, certain descriptive terms will be introduced at the beginning of each section, and where possible the obsolete stitches will be compared to modern stitches that are recognised today. Crucially, diagrams are used throughout the book to clarify the structures attributed to certain terms, and to illustrate the author's use of terminology.

Part of John Taylor's poem in the 1640 copy of *The Needles Excellency A New Booke wherin are divers Admirable Workes wrought with the Needle. Newly invented and cut in Copper for the pleasure and profit of the Industrious.*

For Tent-worke, Raisd-worke, Laid-worke, Frost-worke, Net-worke,
Most curious Purles, or rare Italian Cutworke
Fine Ferne-stitch, Finny-stitch, New-stitch, and Chain-stitch,
Brave Bred-stitch, Fisher-stitch, Irish-stitch, and Queen-stitch,
The Spanish-stitch, Rosemary-stitch, and Mowse-stitch,
The smarting Whip-stitch, Back-stitch, & the Crosse-stitch.

A list of stitches found under the School Mistress's list of terms in Randle Holme's (1688) *The Academy of Armory.*

Plat=Stitch, or finger Plat Stitch, which is good on one side.
Plat=Stitch or double Plat=Stitch, which is alike on both sides.
Spanish stitch, true on both sides.
Tent=stitch on the Finger.
Tent=stitch on the Tent.
Irish stitch.   Back=stitch.
Fore=stitch.   Queens=stitch
Gold=stitch.   Satin=stitch.
Tent=stitch   upon Satin.
Fern=stitch.   Finny=stitch.
New=stitch.   Chain=stitch.
Bread=stitch.   Fishers=stitch.
Rosemary=stitch.   Mow=stitch.
Whip=stitch.   Cross=stitch.

Working Methods

As already mentioned, although one can be certain of the structure, it is not possible to know the exact way in which the original stitches were worked. The start and end of the stitch structure can be deduced from clues such as overlapping or pierced stitches, but the angle of working is more elusive. Lines of stitches can be created vertically, horizontally or at a slant. Indeed, a flexible approach can be advantageous as one works around the contours of a design. However in order to maintain consistency, the stitches in this book are shown worked vertically, from bottom to top, and left to right. The working procedure is an assumption, and illustrates just one potential method. Nonetheless, this decision has been influenced by circumstantial evidence. For instance, indications can be found by observing the way the stitches tend to cross over one another. This is best illustrated by considering the loops created when making stitches such Ladder and Ceylon stitches. Although the number of loops in each row varies, the action is the same throughout. Whilst it is possible to work these loops in either direction, one way is more comfortable than the other. The consistent difference between the modern and Elizabethan versions can be seen in the way in which the loops cross over themselves. Modern stitches are usually shown with an S-crossing. These stitches are worked downward from left to right, so an S-cross is naturally formed as the thread passes over itself from left to right. In contrast to the modern versions, the examples found on the old textiles have Z-crossings. This small structural difference implies that the stitching was worked using a different method. Z-crossings will form if the rows are worked from right to left, but this is not a comfortable process for right-handed stitchers. Another awkward method of making a Z-crossing is to take the thread under itself, rather than over. However, a more effective alternative is to work the stitches upwards, away from the stitcher, and from left to right. The ease at which the stitch structures are recreated in this manner leads one to consider this as the preferred method. It is for these reasons that the stitches are all shown worked in this way.

An additional advantage of working in a bottom-to-top direction is that the hand of the worker is less likely to cast a shadow over the work in progress.

With regard to lighting, modern embroiderers often comment about the difficulties they assume their predecessors faced. However, even in Elizabethan times daylight had long been recognised as a necessity for producing superior work, and in the author's opinion electric lighting is no substitute for working during daylight hours.

The stitches are shown using the *stab* method, rather than *sewing*. This means that the needle passed through the fabric just once every movement, going from above the fabric to below the fabric, or visa versa. This differs from sewing where the needle passes through the fabric twice in the same action, so that the needle remains on the surface of the fabric. The stab method is usually used when the fabric is stretched on a frame, as is not pliable enough to allow the needle to pass through twice. The sewing method is faster compared to the two passages required of the stab method. However, when working on fabric that is held taut on a frame, the stab method is more likely to produce a better quality result. In addition, it has the advantage of being less abrasive, a significant advantage when using expensive threads. Although one can re-create the historic stitches using sewing style actions, there is plenty of evidence that frames were used during this period, and for all the above reasons the stab method has been selected to illustrate the stitches shown in this book.

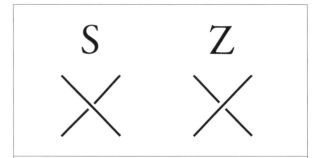

Fig. 2. An S-crossing is when a diagonal line crosses over from top-left to bottom-right, like the slant on a letter S, whilst a Z-crossing slants the opposite way.

Starting & Finishing

The stitches found on surviving textiles exhibited a certain amount of variation on a theme, illustrating a flexible and personal approach to needlework. This is particularly true of starts, finishes and turns, and it was not uncommon to find a variety used within the same piece of work as the stitches were adapted around the design. It is not realistic to illustrate every scenario, so just one option has been selected for each stitch shown in this publication.

Theme and variation also applied to the securing of the thread at the start and end of the stitching. A knot or a series of small extra stitches were usually used to fasten the thread. Sometimes knots were found at both the start and the end of the thread. Some thread ends were found knotted around previous stitching. Threads were also secured with small stitches, often half or running stitch. These were hidden in various ways, such as working them into the linen off the edge of the design, working them into the linen and covering them with subsequent stitching, or by working them into the back of previous stitches. Many starts and ends were avoided by taking the thread from one small section of stitching to another, creating long floating stitches on the reverse of the fabric.

The joining of a new thread was usually done in a similar manner to the start and ending. However, in some circumstances, when it was not possible to take the threads to the back of the fabric, two threads were worked as one before discarding the old thread and continuing with the new.

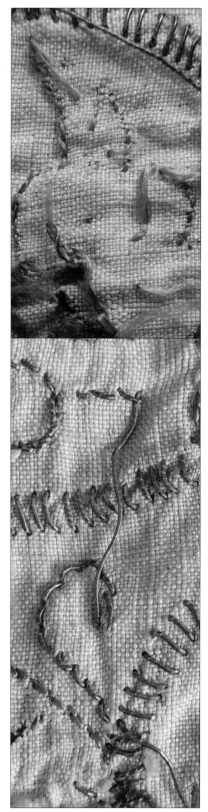

> **Fig. 3. (right)** Detail of the coif in Case Study 22 (page 144). The top image shows the end of the silk taken to the back of a leaf motif and finished with a couple of small stitches. The bottom image illustrates a passing thread making large floating stitches as it travels from one section to another.
> © *Witney Antiques.*

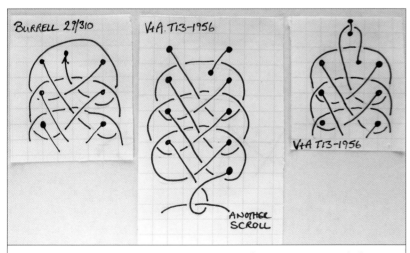

> **Fig. 4.** Surviving itmes exhibited a certain amount of variation. For example, here are just three recorded endings for standard Elizabethan plaited braid stitch.

7

Fig. 5. The reverse of some embroidery from Case Study 12 (page 76) showing the end of a passing thread being secured around the underside of previous stitching. The new thread was started with a knot.
© Privately owned. Copyright in the image reserved to the owner.

Dates

Dating textiles is not an exact science. Occasionally, there are clear indications, such as a year embroidered onto an item (for example, page 55), or strong supporting contextual evidence. However, many statements regarding the age of a textile are assessments based on factors such as composition, pattern and material. These factors can be compared to other more reliably dated objects, documents and portraits (for example, page 92). Unfortunately, it is not always easy to establish cut-off points of when something started or finished. Therefore, it is should be remembered that these assessments are a guide, based on current thinking.

This is also true of trying to date the stitch structures shown in this book. Extant examples were found on items dating from the 16th and early 17th century. A more thorough investigation of examples outside of this period needs to be undertaken to ascertain whether these stitches stem from an earlier period, and to establish when they disappeared from use in Britain. The title *Elizabethan Stitches* was selected because it is the earliest period discussed in this book, even though for various reasons not all the illustrating case studies fall within this era. However, they do have a relationship to earlier items. For instance, the front cover illustrates a panel that might be assessed as early 17th century or Jacobean. Direct comparisons can be made to a jacket in the Victoria & Albert Museum that is currently dated to 1600-25. Yet the development of the style, and examples of the same stitches can be found in earlier pieces. For instance, the heraldic cover (Victoria & Albert Museum T.262-1968) places some of the same stitches more comfortably within the Elizabethan period, as it is associated to a wedding that took place in 1592.

Measurements

Taking measurements of historic artefacts and the materials used in their production is not a straightforward task, as it can entail damaging the object. The measurements used in this book are given as a guide only. They are based on visual observations with a metric tape measure (and are rounded to the nearest inch). In addition, the historic examples have been directly compared with modern materials under a magnifier.

Materials

During the pre-industrial age of the 16th and 17th century, materials would have been processed by hand. Flax, wool and silk fibres were handspun, and coloured by hand-dyeing with natural dyes. Handwoven fabrics were made from handspun threads, then decorated and trimmed by hand. The handmade nature of the whole process resulted in each product having an individual quality. Modern commercially manufactured threads and fabric do not replicate the subtle variations found on historic examples, so ideally reproductions should be made using handmade materials.

> In the 1570s Raphael Holinshed wrote that spinning was one of the accomplishments of ladies in Queen Elizabeth's court, along with languages, needlework and music.

There is plenty of evidence to show that the wealthy Elizabethan households purchased ready-made materials, or hired the services of craftspeople. Alternatively, there is comparable data illustrating that the elite members within the household also undertook the preparation of raw materials. Today however, it is understood that accessing handmade materials is not always practical and that modern alternatives might have to be sourced. Unfortunately, finding commercially produced materials that compare well to the historic examples is a challenge, so one must be prepared to compromise. The following text describes some of the more common materials found on historic examples. It should be noted that in keeping with the survival rate for higher quality items, the materials reflect the more costly end of the market. In an age when all textiles were highly valued, these expensive materials would have provided a visible symbol of wealth. For instance, records show that the average price of metallic threads was three times that of silk. Not only was the cost considerably more than the silk, but the heavy weight of the metal contributed to the fact that an ounce of passing resulted in a much smaller quantity of thread (see Fig. 6). If one considers the fineness of the silk used for needlework, then an ounce of silk equated to a lengthy quantity of thread, and provided far greater coverage than that optained from passing. As a consequence, the use of any metallic thread represented an exceptional extravagance.

The value of embroidery materials may have played a role in shaping the style of stitching. Many of the stitches are relatively simple, especially when compared to later work. Although the results can appear visually complex, they tended to be built up from a few basic movements that were combined and adapted to produce a variety of different effects.

A few selected entries from the 1591-2 household accounts of Nathaniel Bacon.

halfe an ounce of silke	*xijd*
iij qters of silke siprus	*xxjd*
an ounce of blacke silke	*xxijd*
di. ounce of crimson silke	*xiijd*
an ounce of venice gould	*vjs*
ij ounces of fine gould	*xijs*
an ounce of silver thrid	*vs xd*
an ounce of stiffe purle gould	*vjs*
di. ounce of smothe purle gould	*iijs iiijd*
di. ounce of Rugget purle gould	*iijs iiijd*
an ounce of silver purle	*vijs iiijd*
a qter of an ounce of gould plate	*ijs*
ij ounces of gould oes	*xiijs iiijd*

Key:
d = one old penny
12d = 1s = a shilling
20s = li = a pound
1 oz = 1 ounce = 28.3 grammes
16 ounces = 1lb = one pound weight
di = half
j is used to denote the last i in a roman numeral

Fig 6. An ounce (28.3 grammes) of silk represents a large quantity of thread. The amount is shown here, alongside an ounce of modern silver passing and an empty reel to illustrate the extent of the thread.

The emphasis of the historic work tended towards the economic use of materials. Generally, very little thread is wasted on the reverse of fabric, where it is hidden from view, whilst the surface sections are enlarged to take advantage of the visual impact. When one considers the expense of the materials, it is not surprising that the embroiderers would want to make the best use of it.

Fabrics

Linen

Flax was a commonplace material, used in all walks of life. When processed into an undyed linen fabric it formed the base for many needlework projects. Surviving examples are usually worked on a fabric of plain-weave structure (also known as *tabby*). A fabric made from fine and tightly woven threads tends to be found as a base for the decorative embroidery that only partially covers the fabric. In contrast, the base fabric for silk needlepoint is typically seen to be a more open and slightly coarser plain weave fabric. Here, the intersections of the warp and weft provided the grid over which the needlepoint stitches are worked. The handwoven fabric, made from fine Z-twisted threads, is rarely even. Consequently, the grid size tends to fluctuate within a single piece of fabric making the stitch sizes inconsistent. However, many of the opulent examples are so fine, with the linen equating to at least a 35-count* canvas in modern materials, that such variance is barely discernable. Working in tent stitch, a typical piece would require over 1225 stitches to cover a square inch. Today, this might seem excessively fine, but one has to remember that textile skill was commonplace, and learnt from an early age. When this factor is combined with the importance placed on quality, it is not surprising that the linen count is so high, as this would provide the grid for more elegant needlework designs.

When working needlepoint into a linen fabric it is necessary to find a suitable gauge of thread. If the thread is too thick it will start to compact the linen weave, making it so tight that it becomes unworkable. There is evidence of this in some historic pieces, as well as the clue to the solution - after a small section of increasingly dense needlework, the embroiderer changed the thread for a finer one !

Silk

A more sumptuous base fabric for decorative embroidery was made from silk, typically woven in a satin structure so that the fine floating threads created a lustrous sheen. This silk satin was obviously valued, as several small purses were found with seamed joins in the fabric, suggesting that even small snippets were utilised.

Early examples of silk satin are often a rich red colour that forms a contrasting background to the metallic threads used on their surface. White satin appears more frequently on later pieces, particularly when used as a background for embroidered pictures. A more common silk fabric, known as *grosgrain*, can also be found on surviving items. This fabric is a plain weave structure made from fine warp threads and a thicker weft, resulting in a ribbed effect. It is typically found being used as a lining fabric, and is frequently salmon pink in colour.

Other fabrics

Decorative stitching can also be found on other fabrics such as velvet and leather. Velvet was a costly material and formed a particularly opulent contrast to metallic embroidery. Whilst the robust nature of leather was an advantage when making accessories such as gauntlets, passing a needle through the stiff fabric meant that the needlework was more difficult and time consuming. In spite of this, some exquisite examples of decorative embroidery can be found on leather bases.

Fig. 7. Close-up detail of plain-weave linen fabrics (tightly woven on the left, and a more open weave on the right). Note the somewhat irregular Z-twisted threads.

*Count (ct)refers to the number of threads along a linear inch of the fabric.

Threads

Silk

A fine 2-ply S-twisted silk thread was found serving many purposes on the surviving textiles. This type of thread was used in the construction of trimmings and tassels, and also formed the inner core of metallic threads. It was found used for sewing seams and couching work, as well as for some embroidery. However, most of the embroidery was worked in a flossy silk, with little or no twist. Straight fibres produce a more lustrous appearance, and help to provide good coverage, because the stitches are flatter and wider than those made with plied silk. Practical experiment found that in order to replicate the fine scale of work seen in original needlepoint, one would have to use at least a 600 denier* flossy silk, worked over a 35ct linen, though many examples were even finer than this.

A similar silk was also used for the looped stitches. It is thought that the flossy fibres would have been conditioned, to help keep them smooth and more managable as the needle frequently passed through the stitching, and would pierce the thread even when working with a blunt tipped needle.

Metallic

Some surviving items were heavily encrusted with metallic threads and these would have represented an enormous investment of wealth. Even small features made from metallic thread were highly valued, and would have provided an eye-catching detail on any object. Metallic threads, made by combining metal with silk or linen, were found applied in different ways. They were used extensively in the production of tassels, edgings and other trimmings. They were also used for decorative embroidery, either couched down onto the fabric's surface with a separate thread, or stitched directly into the fabric.

A wide range of different metallic threads was found on the surviving objects. The most common is known today as *passing,* or *filé.* This comprises a core thread tightly wrapped with a thin flat strip of metal making the inner core barely visible. The historic examples were made from metal strips S-twisted around silk, though linen cores have also been found. Today, the historic threads are tarnished making it difficult to detect the original colour, and to appreciate the full impact that the shiny thread would have had. The silver metal strips were often seen wrapped around a white silk. Yellow silk was often found for the core thread of gold strips. These strips are not pure gold but gilt, made from a process that adheres a thin layer of gold foil onto another metal, usually silver.

Many variations of passing were found. Sometimes the wrapping of the flat metal strip was deliberately elongated to expose some of the inner core. Here, the silk core was usually a bright colour that would add a hue to the overall

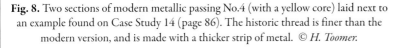

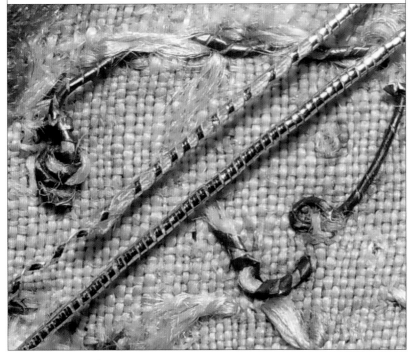

Fig. 8. Two sections of modern metallic passing No.4 (with a yellow core) laid next to an example found on Case Study 14 (page 86). The historic thread is finer than the modern version, and is made with a thicker strip of metal. © *H. Toomer.*

* Denier = a measure of silk thickness equal to the weight in grams of 9000 metres of thread

product. The wrapping could be elongated just a little, or exaggerated to reveal a more intense colour. Another less common version of the elongated passing was produced by wrapping the core with wire that has a round cross-section, rather than a flat strip, thus creating a subtly different texture (see Fig. 9).

Unfortunately, the historic metallic threads are difficult to imitate. Today, most metallic threads are made using a shiny synthetic material, so they work quite differently to the ones that were available in the 16th and 17th centuries. Passing made from solid metal strips is more robust than the synthetic versions, and as a consequence it is easier to work with. Modern passing made from real metal strips is commercially available, but it does not fully replicate the original types found on early pieces. This is partly due to the composition of the metal. Early metallic threads were made from various metals and alloys, but today the metal content is uniform. A more significant factor is the scale of the thread. On the whole, the older threads tended to be much finer than those available today.[*] Although the overall thread was finer, the metal strip wrapped around the core thread tended to be much wider and thicker than present-day versions, possibly due to less sophisticated means of flattening the wire when making the metal strips. Indeed, in some cases the size and shape of the strip was found to vary even along a single thread. These differences in the make up affects the solidity of the thread, and the way in which it bends.

There is often a concern that the outer wrapping on a passing thread will shred during the stitching process. This risk can be reduced by minimising abrasive actions, such as applying the stab method (see page 6). Another helpful tip is to work with a large blunt-ended needle that forces the fabric wide apart before the thread is pulled through. However, it should be noted that synthetic metallic threads are more prone to shredding than those made from precious metals. The historic examples displayed comparatively little evidence of the wrapping detaching from the core, except at the ends when it appeared to have been deliberately removed to assist with securing of the thread. It is possible that the thicker metal content of the historic passing made the thread more robust and reduced the prob-

lem. However, the issue remained, and when a thread did get damaged during the stitching, two large floating stitches were used at the back to 'take-up' the damaged section.

Ornaments

Cord
Different ornaments were used to embellish the needlework. These were usually couched down with a separate thread, rather than used to make the actual stitches. Cords were a common form of ornament. They were generally a narrow 2-ply cord, with each ply comprising a single passing thread. However, a variety of other combinations were also found couched down onto fabric.

Purl
The term *purl* refers to a coil of metal wound into a narrow spring-like shape. Today, styles of purl are standardised, and identified with specific terms. However, the historic examples were found to vary, not just in cross-section but also in scale. Like the metal strips used for the passing, the dimensions could vary along a single length, especially in the older examples (for example Case Study 8). Many different gauges were found, both

Fig. 9. Close-up of a pansy found on Case Study 4 (page 52). The thread is a blend of coloured silk wrapped in a round wire. The coils are loosely wound, though in some places they are more concentrated. A single freshwater pearl has been stitched down at the centre of the pansy.
© Embroiderers Guild.

[*] Usually, the finest commercially available passing is size No.4, but many historic examples were found to be size No.3 or finer.

in the width and thickness of the metal and in the diameter of the coil. However, the coils fell into two distinctive types: those made from round wire, with a circular cross-section (see Fig. 57), and those made from a flattened wire to create a flat strip (see Fig. 10). Both types were found elongated to give different textures, and some were even flattened or wrapped to give more unusual effects.

Plate

Here, strips of flat metal are referred to as *plate*. Historic examples were found couched down onto fabric, either laid flat, or with slight indents periodically placed along its length. Different sizes were found, though they were all relatively fine, usually around 2 to 3mm (around ⅟₁₆ inch) in width.

Oes and Spangles

Pieces of flat metal were also cut into shapes and stitched down onto fabric to add a glamorous sparkle to textiles. They were found in a range of shapes and sizes, and the methods of attachment varied. Typically, they were disc shaped with a hole at the centre. Although they are similar in appearance to

Fig. 11. A close-up of a *spangle* or *oe* from Case Study 12 (page 76). © *Privately owned. Copyright in the image reserved to the owner*

modern sequins, these historic discs tend to be flat, rather than domed. In addition, they would have been cut, rather than stamped, out of the metal. This is evident from the distinctive slit that often widens into a V-shape on the outer rim. This feature was formed whilst cutting from the outer edge to the inner hole. Today, reproduction flat discs are usually referred to as *spangles* in order to differentiate them from modern sequins, and this term is also used to identify the historic examples. However, evidence suggests that the word was used differently in a historical context, and they were originally called by the obsolete term of *oes*.

Miscellaneous

A wide range of other items was used to embellish the needlework. Items such as small glass beads or seed pearls provided highlights among the stitches (see Fig. 9). More unusual materials, couched down to create interesting effects, included human hair and feathers.

Fig. 10. A detail from Case Study 4 (page 52), showing three different types *purl* have been couched down on the fabric.
© *Embroiderers Guild.*

Equipment

The basic tools required by an embroiderer are few: needle, frame and scissors. In Randle Holme's encyclopaedic *The Academy of Armory* he lists the terms, tasks and equipment associated with various trades. Though written slightly later than the period discussed in this book, the school mistress's list gives us a sense of the things that were considered necessary for a woman to produce small textile projects (see boxed text).

Frames

The existence of embroidery frames, known as *tents*, can be seen from inventories and pictorial evidence dating from the 16th and 17th century. Randle Holme listed the parts of the 'Working Tent, or Straining Frame' under the embroiderer's tools. As the evenness and quality of stitching is improved when the base fabric is held taut and fixed, it is advisable to use a frame whilst reproducing most of the needlework illustrated in this book.

Needles

According to records, the craft of needle-making was known in Elizabethan England. Holme gives a list of many kinds of needle, but it is not known exactly which type of needle would have been selected for specific needlework tasks. Practical experiment has demonstrated that a modern tapestry needle gives the best results for the needlepoint and most of the embroidery. This is because the rounded end allows the needle to slip between the threads rather than pierce and split them. It was also discovered that a relatively large needle helped, particularly when working with metallic threads. A needle that is marginally larger than the holes between the weave helps to push open the space between the linen threads. This increases the size of the hole through which the embroidery thread has to pass, and reduces the friction on the fibres. It also adds to the distortion of the linen weave, a characteristic seen in extant examples. Blunt needles were also found to be more efficient when stitching the raised work, as they easily passed between the previous stitches rather than snagging on the thread. The presence of pierced fabric and thread suggests that sharp needles were used in some instances, such as when couching down purl, and for attaching the trimmings.

Scissors

Interestingly, Holme does not mention scissors, although they or a sharp blade would have been needed to cut the thread.

In 1688, Randle Holme published *The Academy of Armory, or, storehouse of Armory and Blazon*. In it he details 'The School Mistris Terms, and things to work with', which includes the following:

Needles, of several sizes.
Cruel of all colours.
Silk for sowing of all colours.
A Tent.
A Samcloth, a cloth to sow on, a Canvice cloth.
Slave Silk.   Naples Silk.
Fine white Alcomy Wyre.
Ising Glass,   Gum Arabick. Gum Dragon.

He also elaborates on the description of a tent...

In the Working Tent, or Straining Frame, there are these parts.
The Frame or Straining Tent.
The Mortised pieces, which have square holes cut through at each end.
The Running pieces, which go through the Mortises, to make the Frame wider or closer together.
The Holes and Pins, they hold it at its distance.
The ------ or Lift about the Imbrauthered work.
The Pack thread, by which it is strained.

Designs

The designs ornamenting the surface of surviving textiles are varied, but many have similar themes. Generally, the colour schemes were bold, and many are enhanced with the abundant use of metallic threads and ornament. Today, the metals are tarnished, and the silks often faded from exposure to light, but once they would have been visually striking pieces.

Many authors have mentioned the strong link between flowers and Elizabethan embroidery. The enthusiasm for flowers was widespread, and it was not limited to their medicinal and aromatic properties. Domestic gardens flourished in the late sixteenth century, and there was a growing interest in botany. Many new flowers, such as the tulip, were introduced into England. So perhaps it is not surprising that floral designs had particular appeal during this period, with embroidery reflecting the fashion for gardens. The visual link between gardens and textile design can be observed in the painting of Lettice Newdigate at Arbury Hall (see Fig. 12).

The floral designs found on surviving textiles typically feature certain flower types. The rose was a

Fig. 12. A portrait of Lettice Newdigate, aged two. It was painted by an unknown artist in 1606. The detail, left, shows the knotwork pattern on the child's stomacher and echoes the design seen in the formal garden viewed through the window. *With kind permission of Lord Daventry.*

particularly popular motif, as was the pansy (also known as *hearts ease*), honeysuckle (*woodbine*), carnation (*gilliflower*), cornflowers and borage. Grapes, strawberries and peapods also make frequent appearances. The floral designs tend to be densely packed, with the spaces between the flowers filled with buds, leaves and fauna motifs, usually consisting of butterflies, caterpillars (or worms) and birds. The motifs were not worked to scale, a feature that is typical of embroidery from this period.

Floral motifs appear as small independent sprigs, sometimes interspersed with fauna, or set within a geometric framework. However, a popular form of patterning is a coiling stem design, sometimes referred to as *scroll work* or *rinceaux*. It consists of large floral motifs, connected with coiling stems, with small leaves, buds or tendrils attached. The stems are usually worked into circular forms surrounding each large flower. Other smaller motifs, either floral or fauna, are sometimes added to fill any spaces. Although few garments survive from the Elizabethan period, these floral arrangements can be seen in portraiture from the era. For example, a portrait of Elizabeth Cornwallis, Lady Kyston dating from 1573, shows her wearing sleeves with the coiling stem design depicted in blackwork. The design style can be found more readily on surviving artefacts thought to date from the early seventeenth century. It was obviously a popular form of patterning and it can be found on a range of items, worked a variety of different techniques.

More abstract patterns also played a part in textile design. A style known as *Arabesque* or *Moresque* was fashionable in the 16th and 17th century. These stylised swirling patterns were inspired by Islamic art, and their influence can be seen on textiles and in portraits, such as the one of Queen Elizabeth I in the National Portrait Gallery (NPG 2471). The use of geometric designs was also widespread, and they were typically based on a diagonal lattice framework, sometimes referred to as a *diaper* pattern. The latticework often encloses small floral motifs within the central spaces. Once again, the popularity of these designs can be seen on surviving textiles from the period, as well as in portraits, such as seen in Fig. 12.

Design Sources

The outline of the design, marked in black ink on the linen fabric, is still visible on many surviving textiles (see Figs. 13 and 49). The motifs are in a simplified form, and as drawing often formed part of a young lady's education, it is possible that these outlines were drawn directly onto the linen, inspired by actual flowers or from memory. Records imply that this was sometimes the case. For example, Mary, Queen of Scots' 1586 inventory recorded "52 different flowers in petit-point drawn from life," and Lady Bridget Vere wrote that "the working of slips, it is some part of our daily exercise, and the drawing of them." Abbot de Fenelon included painting amongst his recommendations for a gentlewoman's education, saying that it "is peculiarly allowed to Women; without it their Works can hardly be well manag'd."

In addition, the outlines could have originated from other sources. Although books were still relatively rare and expensive, the development of the printing press had made them more accessible. This material provided the inspiration for many embroideries and some textiles can be directly linked to certain publications.

Herbals and emblem books

It appears that some floral embroidery designs originated from herbal books, as many were illustrated with images of flowers and herbs. Even though these prints were not intended for embroidery designs, they could

be copied onto fabric for this purpose. Emblem books were another source of inspiration. These popular publications were full of pictures linked to a saying, or moralistic tale. Many books used the same sort of imagery to depict similar stories, so it can be assumed that there was some common understanding of these emblems. The images, with their associated meanings, were also mentioned in contemporary accounts, and some were adopted as personal devices as the mottos were considered to have personal relevance. Some of these emblematic scenes were used as a direct source for embroidery designs, as can be seen from surviving textiles.

Needlework book

The earliest known book printed specifically for needlework was published in Augsburg, in 1523, and the concept then spread to Britain. In 1548, Thomas Geminus published *Morysse and Damashin renewed and encreased very profitable for Goldsmythes and Embroderars* and as the title suggests it was aimed at a specific audience. Another well-known book is Jaques Le Moyne's *La Clef des Champs,* published in London in 1586. His volume of hand coloured woodcuts depicts realistic flowers, animals, insects, fruit, plants and birds. Today, it is difficult to imagine how this could be considered a book for needlework, as there is no mention of any stitches, nor are there any suggestions as to how the images should be interpreted into textile patterns. However, the book's dedication, to Madame Sidney, explicitly suggests that the plates can be used "for embroidery, tapestry and also for all kinds of needlework." In comparison, Richard Shorleyker's (1632) *A Schole-house for the Needle* contains stylised patterns, and some designs are visibly recognisable as textiles. Nonetheless, there is still an assumption of the reader's technical skill as there are no instructions on how to interpret or reproduce any of the patterns. Many of his floral and fauna motifs have been simplified into stylised outlines that provided the ideal template for embroiderers. Indeed, there are surviving textiles that incorporate motifs copied directly from this source. Generally, these sorts of books contained designs that could be adapted and applied to any form of textile. Thomas Treveyon's 1608 Commonplace book is unusual in that it contains some designs that are obviously intended for a specific purpose, with arrangements that have been specifically adapted and shaped to form one of the four panels that make up a night-cap.

Samplers

Another source of inspiration came from samplers, also referred to as *samcloths*. In many ways these were far more informative than printed designs. A stitched sampler was not just a storehouse for motifs, but also retained important information about embroidery techniques. Making a sampler was not just a way of practising and testing out ideas; it also produced a visual catalogue of stitches. Unlike pattern books, these rectangles of linen provided a discernible record of how motifs looked when interpreted in different stitches, materials and colour ways. Although many of the motifs found on surviving samplers are only partially worked, they would have provided sufficient information to enable an embroiderer to anticipate the appearance of the final piece. Samplers were valuable and practical items that could be kept, compared, reused and passed on. It is not surprising to find that they are mentioned in various documents, such as inventories and wills.

Fig. 13. An unworked design of roses drawn onto fabric.
© Privately owned. Copyright in the image reserved to the owner

17

Design Transfer

Counted stitches

The orderly nature of needlepoint requires the number of linen threads to be noted, and working geometric designs could easily have been an extension of this concept. Some geometric designs did follow regular arrangements, as the number of stitches in each pattern repeat is uniform, suggesting that stitch counting was used to make an accurate design. However, when the 'same' designs are analysed, it can be seen that the floral motifs are not identical because there are subtle differences in the number and positions of the stitches. Therefore, one can then assume that these designs were not transferred from a pattern or sampler by counting each square on the linen canvas, in the way that graph paper designs are used today

Marked Outlines

The use of black lines marking out a design on the background fabric can be seen on many surviving items, and these would have provided the guidelines for the decorative needlework. There are several ways in which designs can be marked onto the fabric. There is evidence of designs being printed directly onto fabric, (such as the coif T.21-1946 in the Victoria & Albert Museum), but others would have been hand drawn. The outlines could have been drawn freehand directly onto the background, or a copy could be made from a design source and transferred onto the fabric.

It is often assumed that historic designs were transferred using a method called *prick and pounce*. The first stage is to prick an outline onto paper (or parchment) using a pin. Small pinholes have been found around the borders of some printed images, indicating that they provided a design source. If a blank sheet of paper is placed under a printed page, a fine pin can be pushed through the two sheets of paper at intervals around the outline of the motif (see Fig. 14). The small holes leave the original image relatively unscathed whilst indenting the outline onto the other sheet. The same method can also be used to copy an outline from a sampler.

Pouncing is a somewhat messy and inexact method of transferring this outline onto fabric. The pinholes need to be enlarged beyond the size of those found on surviving documents, as the paper is laid on top of the linen and a fine powder pushed through the holes onto the fabric. The dots of powder on the linen can then be connected up with an inked line. A far simpler way is to transfer the design using a light source. Firstly, the copied outline needs to be emphasised by connecting up the pinholes with an inked line (see Fig. 15). This

> Alessandro Paganino's (1527) *Libro Primo* illustrates women using various methods of transferring designs. They include the use of a candle, and a window as a light source.

enhanced outline can be traced directly onto the linen by placing the copy behind the fabric and holding the two up against a light source. (see Fig. 16).

Fig. 14. The outline of a design can be transferred onto another sheet of paper by pushing a pin through the original design and into a blank sheet placed underneath.

Fig. 15. The pinholes in the copy sheet can be emphasised by connecting them together with an ink line.

Fig. 16. The design can be transferred onto linen by placing the paper behind the fabric and holding the two up against a light source. This example shows how clearly an outline can be seen through a fine 35ct linen held up against dull daylight.

Needlepoint

The first group of stitches can be referred to as *needlepoint* or *canvas work*. They are worked onto a plain-weave fabric, typically linen, with the stitches entering and exiting the fabric at specific points between the weave structure. The majority of these stitches follow a zigzag path with elongated sections on the surface and shorter ones on the underside. Indeed, this conservative use of thread underneath the fabric, whilst maintaining maximum impact on the surface, is a characteristic that distinguishes many of the historic stitches from modern needlepoint. In order to clarify the size of these stitch sections the following notation is used (X:Y) with X and Y representing the number of linen strands crossed over in either a vertical or horizontal direction. An example is shown in diagram below.

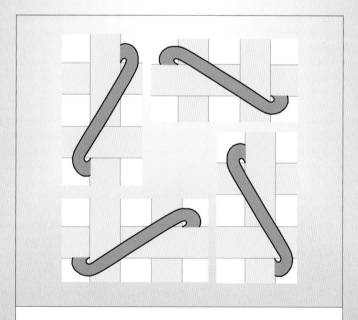

Fig. 17. Each of these four options has a stitch size (1:2) as the stitch section crosses over 1 linen thread in one direction and 2 linen threads in the other direction.

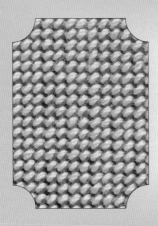

Tent stitch

Today, this is still a popular and well-known stitch, sometimes referred to as *petit point*. Modern stitch dictionaries usually show tent stitch worked in horizontal rows, which results in the structure seen in Fig. 18. Some books offer additional methods, with the stitches worked in diagonal lines. These methods result in the subtly different structures seen in Fig. 19. All versions show the upper section of the stitch with the same covering over the top of the linen, making a Z-slanting stitch. However, the path of the thread under the fabric's surface is different, depending on the angle of the row being worked. The stitch section on the fabric's surface always sits diagonally over one intersection of the linen weave (1:1). Meanwhile the underneath section is either slanted across the linen threads (1:2), or lying parallel to the weave (0:2).

One of the predominant features of Elizabethan needlepoint is the economy of thread used on the underside of the fabric. Tent stitch is the exception as the quantity of the thread on the back is greater than that on the front. It is possible to create the same surface stitch whilst using less on the back, and this stitch is known as *half stitch* (see Fig. 20). However, half stitch has a tendency to flatten itself around the linen weave, resulting in a leaner covering of the fabric (see Fig. 21).

Tent stitch was a very popular stitch and can be found on many surviving items. Some of the larger examples were worked with wool, but most examples were found on a fine linen background fabric, with the stitches worked in silk. Tent stitch provided sufficient

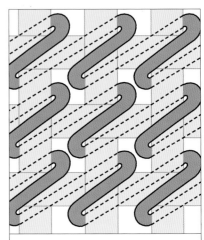

Fig. 18. Structure created by modern tent stitch worked horizontally.

cover over the fabric, yet retained the ability to create dainty designs. With a background plain weave often equating to a 35ct canvas or finer, many tiny stitches were required to cover a square inch. However, it meant that even a small motif such as the pansy seen in Fig. 20 could incorporate complex detail and shading.

In some cases, tent stitch was found entirely covering the linen, with different coloured stitches arranged to create a pictorial design. Sometimes the stitches were used more sparingly. In these circumstances, the stitches were usually employed to fill in motifs that sat on a background covered with another stitch. Tent stitch was also used in conjunction with 3-dimensional motifs, providing a small border edge. This provided a base that was partially obscured under the 3-dimensional stitching as it lifted off the fabric (see Fig. 159, page 150).

Tent stitch motifs are usually outlined with black silk, though this is not always evident, as it has

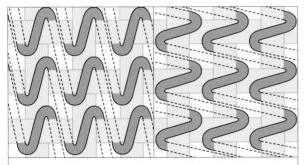

Fig. 19. Structure created by tent stitch, worked diagonally

often perished due to the iron mordant used in the dye. The interior of the motif is then filled with tent stitch worked in various colours. The fact that tent stitch is recognised as the 'same', despite the variations on the back, suits the nature of the stitches found on historic textiles. The designs are usually small and multicoloured, so one does not often find large areas of uniform work. Instead, the stitches are worked in rather haphazard directions. The original stitches tend to be fairly smooth, with a minimum of twist on the flossy silk. This creates small, oblong shaped stitches on the surface of the linen. When pictorial motifs are viewed upright, the stitches were found to be lying in either an S or Z-slant, though some pieces exhibited stitches at both angles. When mixed stitches were found, they usually appeared in random sections, as if there had been an unintentional change of direction. Altering ones working position at the frame can cause this. The same stitching can appear to switch from Z to S, or visa versa, when the frame is turned 90 degrees. However, it seems that some embroiderers were obviously aware of the difference and intentionally changed the angle of their work to create subtle design features.

An example of tent stitch is illustrated in Case Study 1 (page 45).

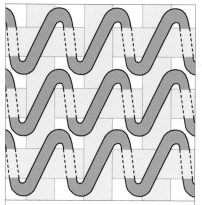

Fig. 20. Structure created by modern half stitch

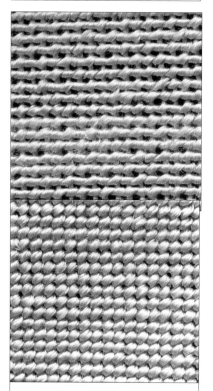

Fig. 21. Tent and half stitch both cover the surface of the linen in a (1:1) sized stitch. However, the tent stitch (lower image) creates a fuller effect compared to half stitch (upper image).

Fig. 22. A small pansy (or heartsease) motif from Case Study 1 (page 45) measuring less than 3cm (1 inch). It has been worked in tent stitch using many colours of silk.
© *Privately owned. Copyright in the image reserved to the owner*

Stitching

The irregular shape of the historic motifs means that a certain amount of flexibility is required when reproducing designs of this type. The motifs rarely follow straight lines, and as a consequence, the order and angle of the stitching varies. Unfortunately working with this kind of irregular action means that it is all too easy to start out making tent stitches, only to discover that one has reverted to half stitch, and that the silk is not fully covering the linen weave. This can be avoided by thinking of the stitch as a form of *back stitch* (Fig.59, page 54). The needle, coming up from below the fabric, needs to do so as far forward of the previous stitch as possible. To make the new stitch, the needle is then taken back towards the previous stitch before entering the fabric. It is not an exact science. Although the surface sections of the stitching will remain the same (1:1), the sections on the back of the fabric will vary, and one should expect a few extra long stitches, and the odd half stitch. There are usually several equally satisfactory ways of filling in a complex motif, so it is a matter of personal taste how one sets about it, a factor borne out in historic examples. The instructions give some options of how one might move on from a Z-slant tent stitch. It should be noted that these are not the only options and that subsequent stitches should be taken into consideration when working a whole motif. For example, Fig. 24 illustrates one potential path around a petal shape, with the numbers denoting the

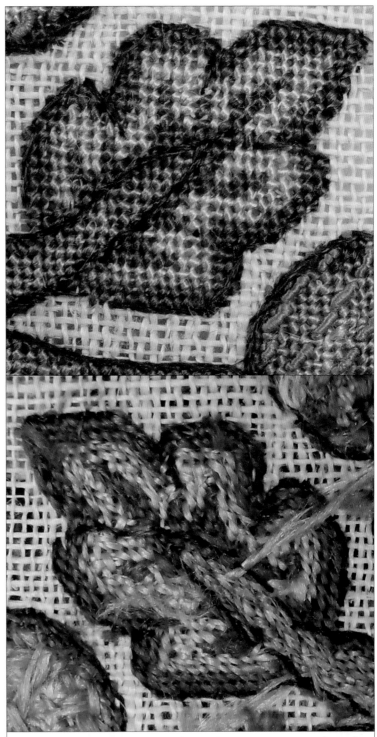

Fig. 23. A detail from Case Study 1 (page 45) showing the back and front of a small leaf motif, worked in tent stitch. Each shade of green follows a meandering course as it works around the contoured area.

22

working order in which the needle exits and enters the fabric. The stitching follows the options shown in the boxed area, with the needle exiting the fabric at the top right-hand corner of the Z-slant stitching. However, the stitch section between 20 and 21 changed the needle's exit point to the lower left-hand end of the Z-slant. This sets up more sympathetic options for the downward part of the circular shape.

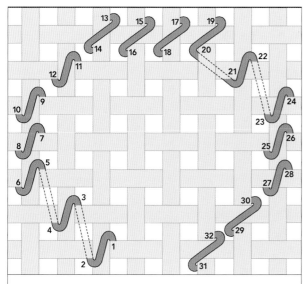

Fig. 24. Tent stitch tended to be worked in rather haphazard directions, and the diagram illustrates the sort of path observed on historic examples. Note that some of the stitch sections below the fabric have been omitted to help with the clarity of the diagram.

Stitching

The first stitch is worked over the surface of the linen exiting from G and entering the fabric at J. The next stitch can be worked using the following options:

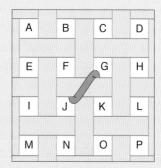

1. Working vertically upwards -
Take the needle underneath the linen (1:2) to C and over the linen (1:1) to F.

2. Working to the top right -
Take the needle underneath the linen (2:2) to D and over the linen (1:1) back into G.

3. Working horizontally to the right -
Take the needle underneath the linen (1:2) to H and over the linen (1:1) to K.

4. Working to bottom right -
Take the needle underneath the linen (0:2) to L and over the linen (1:1) to O.

5. Working vertically downwards -
Take the needle underneath the linen (0:1) to N and over the linen (1:1) to K.

6. Working to bottom left -
Take the needle underneath the linen (1:1) to M and over the linen (1:1) back into J.

7. Working horizontally left -
Take the needle underneath the linen (0:1) to I and over the linen (1:1) to F.

8. Working to top left -
Take the needle underneath the linen (0:2) to B and over the linen (1:1) to E.

Elizabethan reverse stitch

If one works orderly rows of tent stitch, and then turns the fabric over to view the back, one will see Elizabethan reverse stitch. This side of tent stitching exposes more thread on the surface, a common feature of the historic stitching. Examples of both S-slanting and Z-slanting Elizabethan reverse stitch were found on the top surface of some surviving textiles. When worked with metallic passing, the stitch creates an even textured background that provides a good contrast with motifs worked in other stitches. It was also found used as a small highlight when other stitches might seem too complex, such as the shading seen on the book cover (see Case Study 2

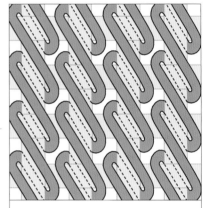

Fig . 25. Structure created by Elizabethan reverse stitch (with an S-slant).

It is possible that the historic examples were the result of tent stitch worked from the reverse of the fabric. Repeats of option 1 on page 23 will produce the S-slant version, whilst repeats of option 3 make the Z-slanting version. However, it has been assumed that the stitching was carried out on the front of the fabric, and the S-slanting version is illustrated here, working a column of stitching vertically bottom-to-top. It is possible to make the subsequent column by rotating the frame a half-turn (180 degrees), so that the stitching can continue progressing in a vertical bottom-to-top direction. However, it is more efficient to master working columns from top-to-bottom, so that the frame can remain static as one works up and down. This is especially useful when making the background between floral motifs, as the columns can be rather short.

Regardless of the method of working, one row is always easier to work than the other. Using the method shown, the downward column is the harder of the two. This is because every time the needle exits the fabric, coming up from below the surface, the space is obscured by the previous stitching (positions F). In contrast, in the alternate columns these spaces are entered from above the surface (positions B), making it is easier to see where one is going. Using a blunt needle should help you to find the space and force apart the linen ready for the new stitch.

An example of Elizabethan reverse stitch is illustrated in Case Study 2 (page 48).

Stitching from bottom-to-top

Step One:
Surface section - from A work over the linen weave 'up 2' and 'left 1', and into B. (When work is under-way, this hole will already contain part of the previous stitching).

Step Two:
Underneath section - from B work under the linen weave 'down 1' and 'right 1', and into C.

Continue repeating the two steps.
Note that position C is position A of the new stitch.

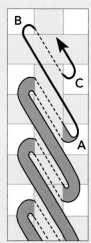

Turning at the top of a column

The last stitch at the top of the upward column is finished partway through the sequence, so that only step one is worked in the usual way. The needle is then taken from B, under the linen 'right 1' to exit at D, ready to start the next column.

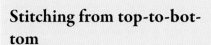

Stitching from top-to-bottom

Step One:
Surface section - from D work over the linen weave 'down 2' and 'right 1', and into E.

Step Two:
Underneath section - from E work under the linen weave 'up 1' and 'left 1', and into F. (When work is underway, this hole will already contain part of the previous stitching).

Continue repeating the two steps.
Note that F is the position D of a new stitch

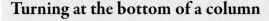

Turning at the bottom of a column

The last stitch at the bottom of the downward column is finished part-way through the sequence, so that only step one is worked in the usual way. The needle is then taken under the linen 'right 1' to exit the linen,

Shaping

When Elizabethan reverse stitch was found creating a back-ground texture, it usually had to work around the contours of the motifs. In these circum-stances, the edges of the stitch-ing rarely ended in a neat straight line. Columns could be shortened or lengthened to help fill the shaped areas. In addi-tion, the turns could be adapted to fit. Here, one needs to elon-gate the section of the stitch that sits under the linen, and angle it so that it comes up to the surface in a position as close as possible to the motif's edge. An example of an elongated turn is illustrated in the diagram below. The underneath section from B works 'up 2' and 'right 1' and into D.

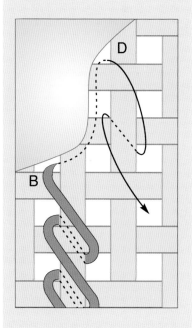

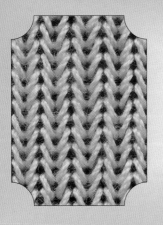

Elizabethan knitting stitch

tudy of surviving textiles revealed that Elizabethan reverse stitch was also worked in alternating columns of S- and Z-slanting stitches. The resultant chevron texture gives rise to Elizabethan knitting stitch. When it is compared to modern knitting stitch (see Fig. 27) one can see that the modern stitch is much larger, with the surface section extending over (1:4) linen threads, rather than (1:2), and the underside reaching over a slant of (1:2) rather than the (1:1) of the old stitch. The petite nature of Elizabethan knitting stitch is even more extraordinary when one considers that the historic examples were generally worked on a finer linen fabric than today's needlepoint.

Working alternate columns of S- and Z-slanting stitches is actually easier than making columns the same slant. This is because when a new stitch connects with the previous column, the needle is always entering from above, rather than coming up from below the fabric, therefore making the space between the linen weave

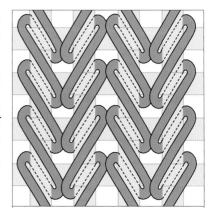

Fig. 26. Structure created by Elizabethan knitting stitch.

easier to find (compare to comments on page 24). Nevertheless, there is one drawback that should be noted. Most stitches are flexible enough for the lines of stitching to be worked together in either direction, but here the turns at the top and bottom of each column have threads entering and exiting out of the same space in the linen weave. This is not an issue when one is working normally because this occurs at opposite ends of the working procedure. However, if for some reason you should start working the opposite way (working the Z-slants bottom-to-top, and S-slants top-to-bottom), then you will soon realise that the turns will not connect neatly together, as the thread tries to simultaneously enter and exit from the same space.

An example of Elizabethan knitting stitch is illustrated in Case Study 3 (page 49).

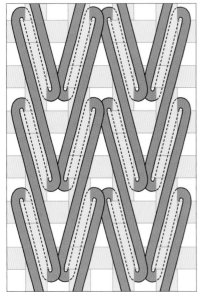

Fig. 27. Structure created by modern knitting stitch.

Stitching from bottom-to-top

This makes a column of S-slanting Elizabethan reverse stitches.

Step One:
Surface section - from A work over the linen weave 'up 2' and 'left 1', and into B

Step Two:
Underneath section - from B work under the linen weave 'down 1' and 'right 1', and into C.

Continue repeating the two steps.
Note that position C is position A of the new stitch.

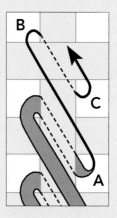

Turning at the top of a column

The last stitch at the top of the upward column is finished partway through the sequence, so that only step one is worked in the usual way. The needle is then taken from B, under the linen 'right 2' to exit at D ready to start the next column.

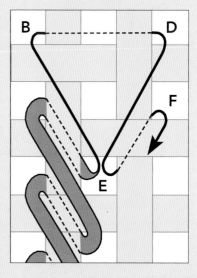

Stitching from top-to-bottom

This makes a column of Z-slanting Elizabethan reverse stitches.

Step One:
Surface section - from D work over the linen weave 'down 2' and 'left 1', and into E.

Step Two:
Underneath section - from E work under the linen weave 'up 1' and 'right 1', and into F.

Continue repeating these two steps.
Note that F is the position D of a new stitch.

Turning at the bottom of a column

The last stitch at the bottom of the downward column is finished partway through the sequence, so that only step one is worked in the usual way. The needle is then taken under the linen 'right 2' to exit the linen, ready to start the next column working bottom-to-top.

Shaping

As with Elizabethan reverse stitch, (page 25), the turns may need to be elongated and angled so that the columns can fit around the contours of other stitching.

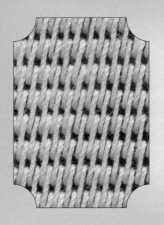

Elizabethan ground stitch

Background areas, filled with metallic passing threads, were usually found to be worked in Elizabethan ground stitch. This popular stitch creates a long slant on the surface and as a consequence it has been mistakenly identified as *Gobelin* stitch (see Fig. 29). Unlike Gobelin, the Elizabethan ground stitch creates a longer slant on the surface, covering (1:4) linen threads. Yet, the biggest difference can be found on the back of the fabric. Here, the surface slants are connected vertically rather than horizontally, with a short section covering just (1:2) linen threads. The resulting stitches resemble modern stem stitch rather than Gobelin, and it is much more economic as the amount of metallic thread used on the back is reduced to a minimum.

One of the characteristics of areas worked in this stitch is the distortion of the underlying linen. Pairs of linen threads are pulled together, creating gaps in the weaving. In the more extreme examples, it is possible to see an object's lining through the spaces. Examination of unworked sections revealed that the distortion is not a woven feature, such as the paired threads found on modern canvases known as *double mesh* or *Penelope*, (page 34) but resulted from working this particular stitch. Practical experiments have indicated that a firm tensioning of the metallic thread is required in order to replicate this attribute.

Elizabethan ground stitch is shown with the slant in a Z-direction, as this was the more usual format, though plenty of S-slant versions were also found, as well as examples that exhibited a bit of both.

An example of Elizabethan ground stitch is illustrated in Case Study 4 (page 52), and Case Study 24 (page 149).

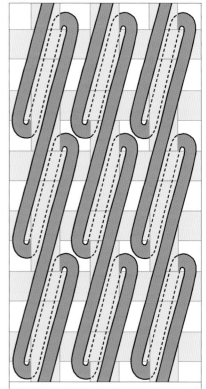

Fig. 28. Structure created by Elizabethan ground stitch.

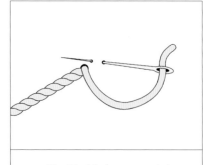

Fig. 30. Modern stem stitch

Fig. 29. Structure created by modern Gobelin stitch

Stitching from bottom-to-top

Step One:
Surface section - from A work over the linen weave 'up 4' and 'right 1,' and into B.

Step Two:
Underneath section - from B work under the linen weave 'down 2' and 'left 1,' and into C.
Continue repeating the two steps. Note that C is the position A of the new stitch.

Turning at the top of a column

The last stitch at the top of column is finished partway through the sequence, so that only step one is worked in the usual way. The needle is then taken under the linen 'right 1' to exit the linen at D, ready to start the next column working top-to-bottom. Alternatively, you can turn the fabric 180 degrees and work another line top-to-bottom.

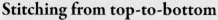

Stitching from top-to-bottom

Step One:
Surface section - from D work over the linen weave 'down 4' and 'left 1,' and into E.

Step Two:
Underneath section - from E work under the linen weave 'up 2' and 'right 1,' and into F.
Continue repeating the two steps. Note that F is the position D of the new stitch.

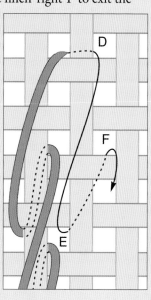

Turning at the bottom of a column

The last stitch at the bottom of the downward column is finished partway through the sequence, so that only step one is worked in the usual way. The needle is then taken under the linen 'right 1' to exit the linen, ready to start the next column working bottom-to-top.

Shaping

As with Elizabethan reverse stitch (page 25), the turns may need to be elongated and angled so that the columns can fit around the contours of other stitching. However, do note that the underneath section will need to travel to the right under one, but up or down under an even number of linen threads (1:even), so that the new line matches the exit/entry points of the previous row.

The lengthy nature of Elizabethan ground stitch means that the tops and bottoms of each column appear sparse. Making the last and/or first stitch of a column a little shorter can help to create a more even covering, and this aspect can be used when shaping an area of stitching. An example is illustrated in the diagram. Here, the turn is elongated and angled, so that the underneath section works 'up 1' and 'right 1'. The top-to-bottom column starts by working 'down 3' and 'left 1', making a shortened stitch and ensuring that the exit/entry points line up with the previous column.

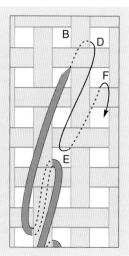

Elizabethan Gobelin stitch

O n the surface of the fabric, Elizabethan Gobelin stitch appears the same as the modern equivalent, covering (1:2) linen threads. However, an important difference can be seen on the reverse of the fabric. The underneath section of the stitch illustrates the economy of thread that is typical of the historic work. Elizabethan Gobelin still forms a zigzag structure with a slanting stitch section on the surface, but the back section lies parallel to the linen weave covering just (0:2) threads, compared to the longer (2:2) section found on modern work. This small change can save around a fifth of the thread needed to cover the fabric. Whilst this might not seem significant today, when one considers the value of materials in the 16th to 17th century (see page 9) this would represent a considerable saving, especially if working with metallic passing. Examples of both S- and Z-slanting stitches were found on surviving textiles. Here, the instructions illustrate the S-slanting version.

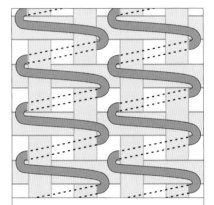

Fig. 31. Structure created by Elizabethan Gobelin stitch.

An example of Elizabethan Gobelin stitch is illustrated in Case Study 5 (page 54).

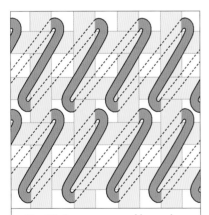

Fig. 32. Structure created by modern Gobelin stitch.

Fig. 33. Top: The front view of Elizabethan Gobelin (on the left) alongside some modern Gobelin (worked sideways so that the stitches align and can be seen to be identical when viewed from the front). **Bottom**: the back view of the stitching showing Elizabethan Gobelin (on the left) and modern Gobelin (on the right), showing the difference in the amount of thread concealed beneath the fabric.

Stitching from bottom-to-top

Step One:
Surface section - from A work over the linen weave 'up 1' and 'left 2,' and into B.

Step Two:
Underneath section - from B work under the linen weave 'right 2' and into C.

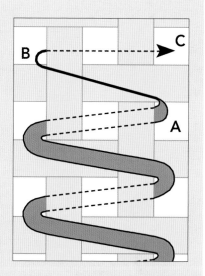

Continue repeating the two steps.
Note that position C is position A of the new stitch.

Turning at the top of a column

No extra instructions are required as position C of the last stitch is the start position of the first stitch in the column worked top-to-bottom. Alternatively, if you turn the fabric 180 degrees to work another line bottom-to-top, then this last position C will be the first position A.

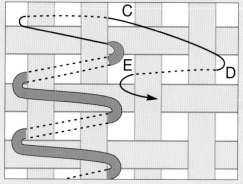

Stitching from top-to-bottom

Step One:
Surface section - from C work over the linen weave 'down 1' and 'right 2,' and into D

Step Two:
Underneath section - from D work under the linen weave 'left 2,' and into E.

Continue repeating these two steps.
Note that position E is position C of the new stitch.

Turning at the bottom of a column

The last stitch at the bottom of the downward column is finished partway through the sequence, so that only step one is worked in the usual way. The needle is then taken under the linen 'right 2' to exit the linen, ready to start the next column working bottom-to-top.

Shaping

As with Elizabethan reverse stitch (page 25), the turns may need to be elongated and angled so that the columns can fit around the contours of other stitching.

Elizabethan plaited Gobelin stitch

Working overlapping columns of S- and Z-slanting Elizabethan Gobelin stitch increases the density of the filling. It is referred to as Elizabethan plaited Gobelin. The historic stitching is like a miniature version of modern plaited Gobelin, as the modern stitch is usually shown covering (2:4) threads on the surface and (0:4) on the back. The smaller Elizabethan version was obviously quite popular as it is found on many items, creating a textured background worked in silk or passing.

Working opposite slants means that the needle is always inserted into the previous stitching from above the surface of the fabric, thus making it easier to find the central gap in the linen between the stitches. However, the needle does not always pass uniformly to one side of the underneath section of the previous column, and can give the reverse side a slightly uneven look.

An example of Elizabethan plaited Gobelin stitch is illustrated in Case Study 6 (page 55).

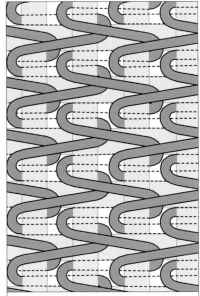

Fig. 34. Structure created by Elizabethan plaited Gobelin stitch.

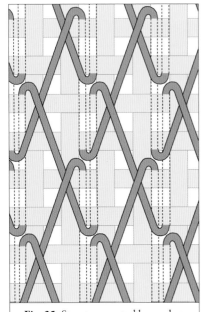

Fig. 35. Structure created by modern plaited Gobelin.

Fig. 36. The reverse view of Elizabethan plaited Gobelin stitch, showing that the back sections can appear a little uneven in places.

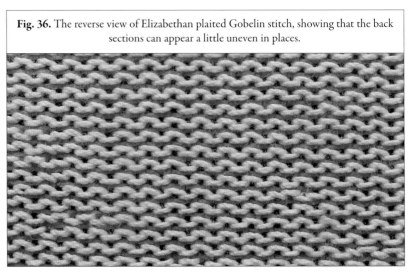

Stitching from bottom-to-top

This creates a column of S-slanting stitches.

Step One:
Surface section - from A work over the linen weave 'up 1' and 'left 2,' and into B. (When work is underway, this will be midway between the Z-slanting stitches).

Step Two:
Underneath section - from B work under the linen weave 'right 2' and into C.
Continue repeating the two steps.
Note that position C is position A of the new stitch.

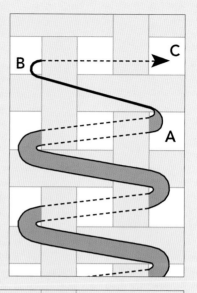

Turning at the top of a column

The last stitch at the top of the column is finished partway through the sequence, so that only step one is worked in the usual way. The needle is then taken under the linen 'right 3' to exit the linen at D, ready to start the next column working top-to-bottom.

Stitching from top-to-bottom

This creates a column of Z-slanting stitches.

Step One:
Surface section - from D work over the linen weave 'down 1' and 'left 2,' and into E. (This will be between the S-slant stitching).

Step Two:
Underneath section - from E work under the linen weave 'right 2,' and into F.
Continue repeating these two steps. Note that position F is position D of the new stitch.

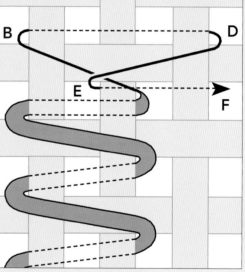

Turning at the bottom of a column

The last stitch at the bottom of the downward column is finished partway through the sequence, so that only step one is worked in the usual way. The needle is then taken under the linen 'right 3' to exit the linen, ready-to start the next column working bottom-to-top.

Shaping

As with Elizabethan reverse stitch (page 25), the turns may need to be elongated and angled so that the columns can fit around the contours of other stitching.

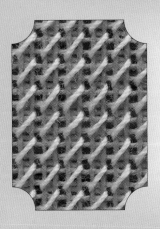

Elizabethan half stitch

Modern half stitch is usually shown with the thread slanting (1:1) on the surface and (0:1) on the back (see Fig. 38). Yet modern references also illustrate it being worked on a canvas known as *double mesh,* or *Penelope.* This canvas fabric is especially woven so that pairs of threads sit close together (Fig. 39). If half stitch is worked on this type of canvas it automatically increases the size of the stitching to (2:2) on the surface, and (0:2) on the back. This spacing is exactly the same as that found on Elizabethan half stitch. Here, the prefix of Elizabethan has been added just to emphasis that it is worked on normal fabric, and the linen threads have to be counted (2:2) in the usual manner. Historic examples were found lying in both a Z and S direction, and just the Z-slant version is illustrated here. Note that like tent stitch, the surface stitches lie on the Z-slant when viewed vertically, but appear S-slant when viewed horizontally.

Like Elizabethan Gobelin, this stitch is rather sparse as a straight-forward filling stitch, so tends to be found combined with other stitches (for example, see page 57). Alternatively, the columns were arranged so that they overlapped one another in a similar manner to Elizabethan plaited Gobelin, giving rise to stitch structures that included modern cross stitch (see page 45) and modern woven plait.

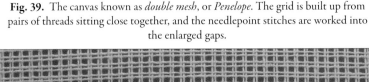

Fig. 37. Structure created by Elizabethan half stitch.

An example of Elizabethan half stitch is illustrated in Case Study 7 (page 56).

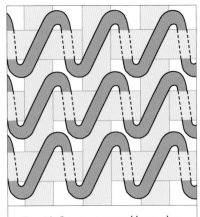

Fig. 38. Structure created by modern half stitch.

Fig. 39. The canvas known as *double mesh*, or *Penelope*. The grid is built up from pairs of threads sitting close together, and the needlepoint stitches are worked into the enlarged gaps.

Stitching from bottom-to-top

Step One:

Surface section - from A work over the linen weave 'up 2' and 'right 2', and into B.

Step Two:

Underneath section - from B work under the linen weave 'left 2' and into C. Continue repeating the two steps.
Note that position C is position A of the new stitch.

Turning at the top of a column

The last stitch at the top of the upward column is finished partway through the sequence, so that only step one is worked in the usual way. The needle is then taken under the linen 'right 2' to exit the linen, ready to start the next column working top-to-bottom.

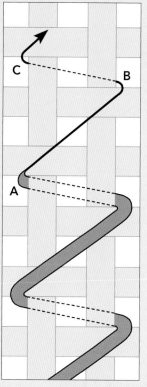

Stitching from top-to-bottom

Step One:

Surface section - from D work over the linen weave 'down 2' and 'left 2', and into E.

Step Two:

Underneath section - from E work under the linen weave 'right 2' and into F.
Continue repeating the two steps.
Note that position F is position D of the new stitch.

Turning at the bottom of a column

No extra instructions are required as position F of the last stitch is the start position of the first stitch in the column worked bottom-to-top.

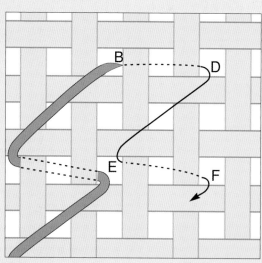

Shaping

As with Elizabethan reverse stitch (page 25), the turns may need to be elongated and angled so that the columns can fit around the contours of other stitching.

Elizabethan half-and-turn stitch

As mentioned on page 34, Elizabethan half stitch was usually found forming part of a composite stitch. These were often composed of columns of stitching connected together in different ways, or added to another type of stitch. Here, the extra components are added between each half stitch, and as a result, the rhythm of stitching is altered. As indicated by its name, an extra turn is added after each half stitch. This extra turn encircles pairs of linen threads, drawing them together so that they distort the underlying fabric. When this stitch is worked with silk, a firm tension can be applied helping to create small gaps in the linen fabric, which add to the net-like quality. The S-slanting version of this stitch is illustrated here, and the method starts with the slanting section of the stitch. Depending on the shaping, you may wish to start and end the columns with either a slanting section, created by the half stitch, or with a horizontal section, created by the extra turn. These can be made by omitting some of the steps in the stitch sequence.

An example of Elizabethan half-and-turn stitch is illustrated in Case Study 8 (page 58).

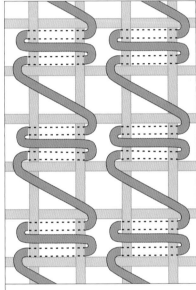

Fig. 40. Structure of Elizabethan half-and-turn stitch.

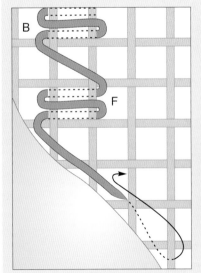

Shaping

As with Elizabethan reverse stitch (page 25), the turns may need to be elongated and angled so that the columns can fit around the contours of other stitching. However, take care to align the stitches to match the exit/entry points of the previous row. This entails starting the turn by going over the linen (at the top of a column), or under the linen (at the bottom of a column) 'right 2' and 'up/down an even number'.

Sometimes it can be useful to omit the extra turn added to the half stitch. This will create a slanted section at the top or bottom of the column, and can help shape the area being filled, as illustrated in the diagram.

Stitching from bottom-to-top

Note that when making the first column, you may wish to start by working step three and four, so that you commence with an extra turn.

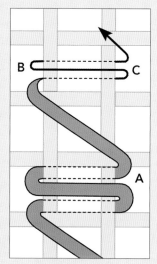

Step One:
Surface section - from A work over the linen weave 'up 2' and 'left 2' and into B.

Step Two:
Underneath section - from B work under the linen weave 'right 2' and into C.

Step Three:
Surface section - from C work over the linen weave 'left 2', and back into B.

Step Four:
Underneath section - from B work under the weave 'right 2', and back into C.
Continue repeating the four steps.
Note that position C is position A of the new stitch.

Turning at the top of a column

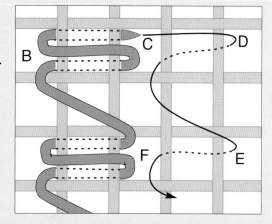

At the top of the column, finish at the end of the sequence. The needle is then taken from C over the linen 'right 2' into D. Then work underneath the linen 'left 2' and back into C. You are now ready to start working a column top-to-bottom. Alternatively, you can turn the fabric 180 degrees and work another line bottom-to-top.

Stitching from top-to-bottom

Step One:
Surface section - from C work over the linen weave 'down 2' and 'right 2' and into E.

Step Two:
Underneath section - from E work under the linen weave 'left 2' and into F.

Step Three:
Surface section - from F work over the linen weave 'right 2', and back into E.

Step Four:
Underneath section - from E work under the linen weave 'left 2', and back into F.
Continue repeating the four steps. Note that position F is position C of the new stitch.

Turning at the bottom of a column

The last stitch is finished partway through the sequence, so that steps one, two and three are worked in the usual way. The needle is then taken from E under the linen 'right 2' to exit the linen. Bring the needle over the linen 'left 2' and back into E, then underneath the linen 'right 2' to exit the linen, ready to start the next column of bottom-to-top stitches

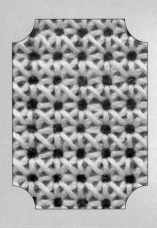

Elizabethan square net

The visual appearance of Elizabethan square net is somewhat similar to the modern stitch known as *raised honeycomb filling*. However, the historic version is more economic, and is built up using Elizabethan half-and-turn stitch. The final stitch is constructed from two layers of this stitch, resulting in crossed surface sections bordered on all four sides with straight lines. The layers of stitching are repeatedly worked into the same spaces between the linen threads, until a total of eight threads enter or exit from the same hole. This increases the distortion in the weave, forcing pairs of linen threads together and widening the gaps between them, thus enhancing the net-like structure.

The two layers can be worked on top of one another in various ways, though they look the same on the reverse of the fabric. Generally, areas of Elizabethan square net are worked in blocks, with the initial stitching covered in a second layer worked at right angles to the underlying layer. In some cases, a combination of S- and Z-slanting stitches were used resulting in an inconsistent structure. For instance, alternating columns of S- and Z-slanting stitches in both layers will result in a checkerboard arrangement of crossed sections and same-slanting sections, each boxed in by four turns. However, as the stitching tended to be fine and worked in a flossy silk, this sort of detail is barely noticeable. A more uniform result can be obtained by working all the stitches at the same slant, and turning the fabric 90 degrees before starting the second layer. As with tent stitch (page 21), turning the fabric alters the slant when viewed from the original angle, and means that the second layer will form crossed sections over the first layer. It is the easiest way of working, and the method shown here illustrates the Z-slanting version.

Examples were also seen of working back over a single column using opposite slanting stitches, in

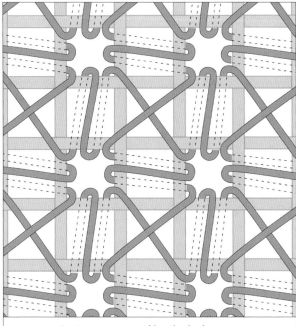

Fig. 41. Structure created by Elizabethan square net.

much the same way that cross stitch is worked (see page 45). This produces crossed sections, but the straight lines are doubled up above and below the cross, leaving the sides empty. Consequently, this style of working tends to be used just for small detail or shaping. An example of Elizabethan square net is illustrated in Case Study 9 (page 59).

Shaping

As with Elizabethan half-and-turn stitch (page 36), the turns can be elongated and angled, but care will be needed to align the stitches to match the exit/entry points of the previous row. The option of omitting the extra turns at the ends of the columns also applies.

Stitching from bottom-to-top

Note that when making the first column, you may wish to start by working step three and four, so that you commence with an extra turn.

Step One:
Surface section - from A work over the linen weave 'up 2' and 'right 2' and into B.

Step Two:
Underneath section - from B work under the linen weave 'left 2' and into C.
(when you are underway, this hole will already contain two threads from the previous column).

Step Three:
Surface section - from C work over the linen weave 'right 2', and back into B.

Step Four:
Underneath section - from B work under the linen weave 'left 2', and back into C.
Continue repeating the four steps. Note that position C is position A of the new stitch.

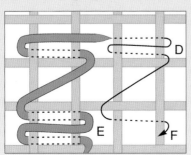

Turning at the top of a column

The last stitch at the top of the column is finished partway through the sequence, so that only steps one to three are worked in the usual way. The needle is then taken under the linen 'right 2' to exit the linen at D. The needle is then taken over the surface 'left 2' and enters the linen, before going underneath 'right 2' to exit again at D. You are now ready to start working top-to-bottom.

Stitching from top-to-bottom

Step One:
Surface section - from D work over the linen weave 'down 2' and 'left 2', and into E (this hole will already contain two threads from the previous column)

Step Two:
Underneath section - from E work under the linen weave 'right 2', into F.

Step Three:
Surface section - from F work over the linen weave 'left 2', and back into E.

Step Four:
Underneath section - from E work under the linen weave 'right 2', and back into F.
Continue repeating these four steps. Note that position F is position D of the new stitch.

Turning at the bottom of a column

No extra instructions are required as position F of the last stitch is the start position of the first stitch in the column worked top-to-bottom.

Second layer

When you have covered an area with the first layer, rotate the fabric a quarter turn (90 degrees) and start working another layer of the same stitching. It is possible to flow from one layer to another. If you end the first layer at the bottom of a column, you will need to turn the fabric clockwise and start a bottom-to-top column (see diagram). Ending the first layer at the top of a column will entail an anti-clockwise quarter turn and the first column of the second layer will be a top-to-bottom one. However if in doubt, turn the fabric either way and simply add a new thread in the bottom left-hand corner and start working upwards.

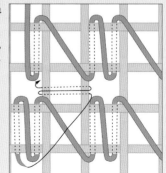

39

Elizabethan Roumanian stitch

The following two stitches differ from the previous ones in that they do not follow a zigzag path. Instead, the thread doubles back over itself resulting in a crossed stitch, with a long surface section pinned down by a shorter section at its centre. These stitches use the grid of the underlying linen as a guide for the exit and entry points, and as such remain part of the needlepoint section. In contrast, modern Roumanian stitch is usually shown worked freely on the fabric, and as with so many of the stitches that cross over themselves, the historic version works in the opposite direction to the modern one. When the stitch is made with flossy silk, the fibres spread over the linen weave and the result is visually similar to the effect created with the Elizabethan Gobelin and back stitches seen in the Case Study 5 (page 54). The nature of the stitch means that the columns end in arrow shapes rather than straight lines. These large stitches do not adapt well to shaping, so are more suited to geometric designs rather than flowing floral ones.

An example of Elizabetathan Roumanian stitch is illustrated in Case Study 10 (page 60).

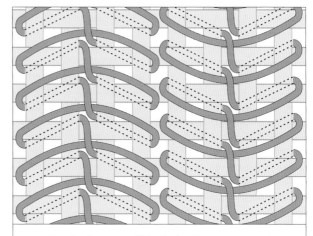

Fig. 42. Structure of Elizabethan Roumanian stitch.

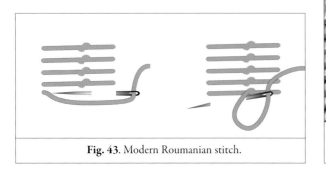

Fig. 43. Modern Roumanian stitch.

Fig. 44. View of the reverse side of the stitching.

Stitching from bottom-to-top

Step One:
Surface section - from A work over the linen weave 'right 4', and into B. Keep the thread a little loose, so that you can easily see where the needle is emerging in step two.

Step Two:
Underneath section - from B work under the linen weave 'up 1' and 'left 2', and into C. Ensure that the needle emerges below the thread AB.

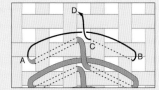

Step Three:
Surface section - from C work over the linen weave 'up 1', and into D. Make sure that the needle goes over the thread AB. Tighten the thread to draw up any slack remaining from step one.

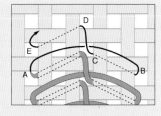

Step Four:
Underneath section - from D work under the linen weave 'down 1' and 'left 2', and into E.
Continue repeating the four steps. Note that position E is position A of the new stitch.

Turning at the top of a column

The last stitch at the top of the column is finished partway though the sequence. Work steps one, two and three ending with the needle entering the fabric at D. The needle is then taken under the linen 'right 6' and 'down 1' to exit the linen at F, ready to start the next column working top-to-bottom. Alternatively, you can turn the fabric 180 degrees and work another line bottom-to-top.

Stitching from top-to-bottom

Step One:
Surface section - from F work over the linen weave 'left 4', and into G. Keep the thread a little loose, so that you can easily see where the needle is emerging in step two.

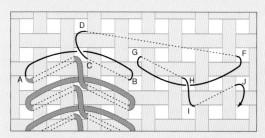

Step Two:
Underneath section - from G work under the linen weave 'down 1' and 'right 2', and into H. Ensure that the needle emerges above the thread FG.

Step Three:
Surface section - from H work over the linen weave 'down 1', and into I. Ensure that the needle goes over thread FG. Tighten the thread to draw up any slack remaining from step one.

Step Four:
Underneath section - from I work under the linen weave 'up 1' and 'right 2', and into J.
Continue repeating the four steps. Note that position J is position F of the new stitch.

Turning at the bottom of a column

No extra instructions are required as position J of the last stitch is the start position of the first stitch in the column worked top-to-bottom.

Shaping

As with Elizabethan reverse stitch (page 25), the turns can be elongated and angled.

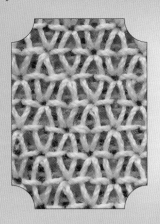

Elizabethan French stitch

Elizabethan French stitch is similar to the previous stitch in that the thread doubles back over itself resulting in a crossed stitch, with a long surface section pinned down by a shorter section at the centre. There are several versions of modern French stitch, and its variation known as *rococo* stitch. However, none of them correspond to this example of Elizabethan French stitch. The visual difference between the Elizabethan and modern versions are subtle on the surface, yet the appearance on the back of the fabric is quite different. The surface of the stitch can be considered as four parts. Two long sections lie parallel to one another, each straddled by a shorter section that lies perpendicular over their centres. The modern versions have shorter sections going from the outer edge of the stitch and entering the fabric into a hole at the centre of the stitch. In contrast, the Elizabethan stitch has both the shorter sections exiting the central hole and working outwards over the longer parts. This has a tendency to spread the stitch into a more circular and symmetrical shape than its modern counterpart. It also dramatically alters the arrangement on the back of the fabric.

The diamond-shaped stitches are usually worked in diagonal lines. The method for working S-slanting line of stitches is illustrated here, although lines of stitching can also be worked in Z-slanting lines. The large stitches do not adapt well to shaping, unless making geometric patterns of tessellating diamonds. Therefore, the stitch does not suit the flowing floral designs.

The following instructions can seem a little long-winded, but once mastered can be summarised by working the diamond shaped stitch *"top-to-bottom, left-to-right, top-to-bottom, right-to-left,"* when working a bottom-to-top column.

An example of Elizabetathan French stitch is illustrated in Case Study 11 (page 61).

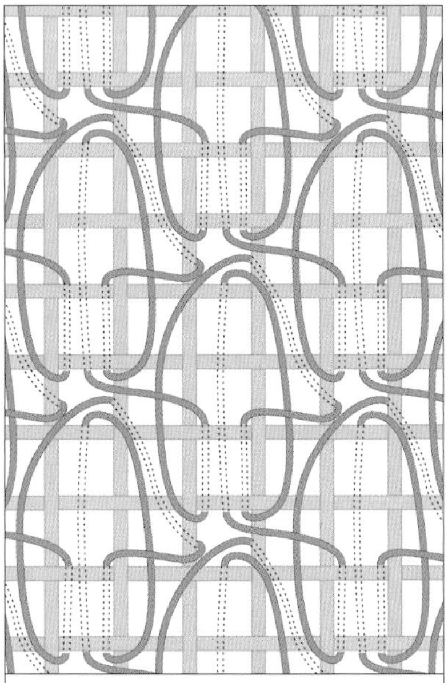

Fig. 45. Structure created by Elizabethan French stitch.

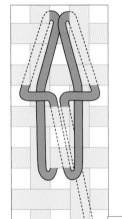

Fig. 46. Structure created by modern French stitch

Fig. 47. Opposite. Detail showing the reverse of Elizabethan French stitch.

Stitching from bottom-to-top

This will make a S-slanting diagonal line of stitches going from bottom-right to top-left.

Step One:
Surface section - from A work over the linen weave 'down 4' and into B. Keep the thread a little loose, so that you can easily see where the needle is emerging in step two.

Step Two:
Underneath section - from B work under the linen weave 'up 2' and into C. Ensure the needle emerges to the left of thread AB.

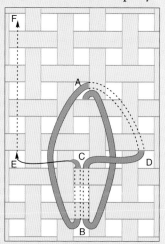

Step Three:
Surface section - from C work over the linen weave 'right 2' and into D. Make sure that the needle goes over the thread AB. Tighten the thread to draw up any slack remaining from step one.

Step Four:
Underneath section - from D work under the linen weave 'up 2' and 'left 2', back into A.

Step Five:
Surface section -from A work over the linen weave 'down 4' and back into B. Keep the thread a little loose, so that you can easily see where the needle is emerging in step six.

Step Six:
Underneath section - from B work under the linen weave 'up 2' and back into C. Ensure the needle emerges to the right of thread AB.

Step Seven:
Surface section - from C work over the linen weave 'left 2' and into E. Make sure the needle goes over the thread AB. Tighten the thread to draw up any slack remaining from step five.

Step Eight:
Underneath section - from E work under the linen weave 'up 4' and into F. You are now ready to start a new stitch. Note that position F is position A of the new stitch.

Turning at the top of a column

Turn just below the require point, as the first stitch of the next line will be slightly higher than the previous line. The last stitch of the bottom-to-top line is finished partway through the sequence, so that only steps one to seven are worked in the usual way. The needle is then taken under the linen 'right 4' to exit the linen at position D. This will be the start position F in the column working top-to-bottom. Alternatively, you can turn the fabric 180 degrees and work another line bottom-to-top.

Instructions continue overleaf.

Stitching from top-to-bottom

Step One:
Surface section - from F work over the linen weave 'up 4' and into G. Keep the thread a little loose, so that you can easily see where the needle is emerging in step two.

Step Two:
Underneath section - from G work under the linen weave 'down 2' and into H. Ensure the needle emerges to the right of thread FG.

Step Three:
Surface section - from H work over the linen weave 'left 2' and into I. Make sure that the needle goes over the thread FG. Tighten the thread to draw up any slack remaining from step one.

Step Four:
Underneath section - from I work under the linen weave 'down 2' and 'right 2', back into F.

Step Five:
Surface section -from F work over the linen weave 'up 4' and back into G. Keep the thread a little loose, so that you can easily see where the needle is emerging in step six.

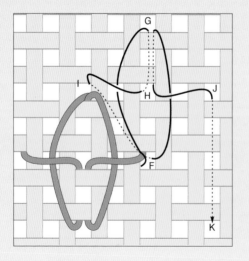

Step Six:
Underneath section - from G work under the linen weave 'down 2' and back into H. Ensure the needle emerges to the left of thread FG.

Step Seven:
Surface section - from H work over the linen weave 'right 2' and into J. Make sure the needle goes over the thread FG. Tighten the thread to draw up any slack remaining from step five.

Step Eight:
Underneath section - from J work under the linen weave 'down 4' and into K.
You are now ready to start a new stitch. Note that position K is position F of the new stitch.

Turning at the bottom of a column

Note that the first stitch of the next line will start slightly higher than the turn. The last stitch of the top-to-bottom line is finished partway through the sequence, so that only steps one to seven are worked in the usual way. The needle is then taken under the linen 'up 4', ready to start the next column working top-to-bottom.

Shaping

As with Elizabethan reverse stitch (page 25), the turns may need to be elongated and angled so that the columns can fit around the contours of other stitching. Care will be needed to align a new column with the exit/entry points of the previous row. It is worth considering the stitch as a diamond shape, with the side points of one column always connecting to the top and bottom points of the adjacent column.

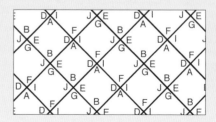

CASE STUDY 1

Example:
Tent Stitch (page 20)
Object:
Panel
Location:
Private Collection

This unfinished panel is thought to date from the late 16th century. It measures approximately 116 cm x 58 cm (46 x 23 inches), so one assumes that it was intended as a furnishing. The all over design consists of floral sprigs each enclosed within a geometric framework filled with strawberry motifs. Around the edge of the panel is a border of coiling stems encircling marigolds and borage. Parts of the design have been outlined with black stitches, and filled with brightly coloured silk needlepoint.

Unfortunately, the black silk has perished in some areas. This is a relatively common phenomenon caused by the iron mordant used in the dyeing process. Interestingly, as the thread has rotted it has revealed that only the sprig motifs are clearly marked out in ink on the fabric. In places, there remains little trace of the framework, except for the distorted holes in the linen weave where the stitches once sat (see Fig. 49).

The sprig motifs are typical of the period, though designs of this type have been used over extended periods of time. Indeed, they are still being reproduced today. There are fourteen different sprigs, repeated randomly within the framework: pansies, borage, marigolds, columbines, foxgloves, daffodils, cornflowers, hazel nuts, acorns, peas, pears, pomegranates, grapes, and another unidentified fruit. Curiously, the rose is conspicuous in its absence. Each sprig is roughly 6 cm square (2 inches) and worked in tent stitch using many different shades of coloured silk. The stitching follows a meandering course as each different colour fills just a small and irregular area within a motif (see Figs. 22 & 23, on pages 21 & 22).

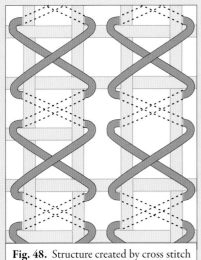

Fig. 48. Structure created by cross stitch

Cross Stitch

Work a bottom-to-top column of S-slanting Elizabethan half stitches (as shown on page 35) except substitute 'left' for 'right' and vice versa. Turn at the top of the column and work back over the stitches with a column of top-to-bottom Z-slanting Elizabethan half stitches (as shown on page 35).

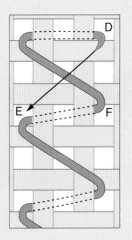

The panel provides a classic illustration of the terms *petit point* and *gros point*. The plain-weave linen has approximately 13-14 threads along a linear centimetre (33 - 35 per inch), so working the entire panel in tent stitch would have been a considerable undertaking. However, the workload was reduced by filling in the bulk of the design using a larger stitch. Here, the sprigs are delicately detailed motifs worked in tent stitch (*petit point*), which covers (1:1) surface threads of the linen weave. In contrast, the framework and border are worked on a larger scale using cross stitch (*gros point*) covering (2:2) linen threads on the surface. Some say that the 'proper' way of making cross stitch is to complete each individual stitch before moving on to the next, but here the cross stitch comprised two lines of Elizabethan half stitch (page 34) worked directly on top of one another, one slanting in an S and the other in a Z direction. The stitches on the panel are not uniform, as both S- and Z-slant stitches were found forming the upper layer of the surface stitch. In addition, stitches worked diagonally created a difference underneath the fabric, much in the same way as described for tent stitch on page 23.

Fig. 50 (Opposite). Part of the unfinished panel, showing the embroidered green geometric framework, filled with strawberry motifs. It surrounds a sprig motif depicting daffodils. Above sits a sprig of grapes and foxgloves that are unworked. A columbine and pear motif disappear into the edge border that depicts coiling stems surrounding borage and marigolds.

© *Privately owned. Copyright in the image reserved to the owner.*

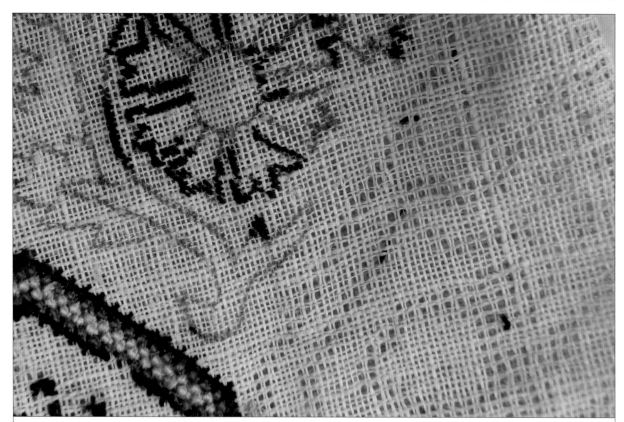

Fig. 49. Detail showing an area where the black silk has perished. The outline of a sprig of cornflowers is clearly marked onto the linen. The existence of the stitching that once formed the geometric framework is evident from the distorted holes in linen weave. It is possible that the faint colouring seen here is a residue of the black dye, or it could be that the framework pattern was marked onto the linen using a different batch of ink that has now faded.

© *Privately owned. Copyright in the image reserved to the owner.*

CASE STUDY 2

Example:
Elizabethan Reverse Stitch (page 24)
Applied Work (page 152 & 153)
Object:
Book Cover
Location:
British Library, London
Shelfmark:
C.65.l.3

This embroidered cover protects *A Booke of Christian Prayers*, which was published in London in 1578 by Richard Day. The book measures approximately 13 cm by 18 cm (5 x 7 inches), with a spine width of approximately 2.5cm (1 inch). A plain-weave linen background envelops the whole of the book's exterior. Originally, two pairs of ties would have secured the front and back cover together, but today only the stump ends are visible at the edge of the fabric. The linen is covered in silk tent stitches, with approximately 8 stitches per centimetre length (20 per inch). Although the colours have faded, they pick out a design of flowers cascading out of a chalice, with an additional rose motif on the left and a lily on the right. Unusally, the image is aligned sideways, so that the spine of the book forms the base of the design.

Each motif is highlighted with a border of metallic threads that have been couched down onto the fabric. Pairs of passing threads either lie parallel to one another, or have been twisted together to form a cord. Metallic passing has also been used to create small areas of shading, notably on the chalice. These areas have been worked in a Z-slanting Elizabethan reverse stitch, though some sections of S-slant stitching can also be found. The shading is a minor detail in the design, but provides a fitting balance to the dainty silk tent stitches.

Fig. 52. The book viewed with the spine along the lower edge. © *British Library Board (C.65.l.3).*

Object:
Sampler
Location:
Embroiderers' Guild Collection, London
Accession Number:
EG 1999.17

CASE STUDY 3

In an age when there was little published material for the embroiderer, the sampler was a valued possession. It was a storehouse of information, recording not just embroidery designs, but also potential stitch options, material guides and colour ways. This particular example is a *spot* sampler, so called because the motifs are randomly scattered across the linen. These differ from *band* samplers that have designs worked in horizontal strips across the linen, and are more typically schoolgirl practice pieces dating from later in the 17th century. This sampler dates from the early to mid 17th century, and one can see from the arrangement and orientation of the motifs that this was not a showpiece, but a reference source for patterns and stitch ideas. For instance, when viewed with the falconer standing upright, some flower sprigs are placed the same way, whilst other flowers sit sideways along the edges, and near the top the letters A to G are upside-down. The random collection of designs also includes repeatable geometric patterns in various stages of completion. It has been noted that similar motifs, such as the falconer, can be seen on other items. This illustrates a shared source of information, and one could speculate that little has changed in an embroiderer's desire to copy an interesting design.

The sampler measures approximately 55 x 22 centimetres (27 x 22 inches), and is made of an open plain-weave linen, with around 12-14 threads per linear centimetre (30-35 per inch). One half of the piece is dominated by designs worked in silk tent stitches, whilst the other half contains more mixed stitches, often worked in metallic passing. In this area is a design of three repeated sprigs, set on a striped background. This is made from Elizabethan knitting stitch, worked in alternate rows of passing and silk.

Fig. 52. The falconer motif is worked mainly in silk tent stitch, though parts of his costume are made from standard Elizabethan plaited braid worked in passing, and small pearls decorate the edge of his hat. The same design has been found on two other samplers, one in the Douglas Goodhart collection and the other in the Smithsonian Cooper-Hewitt Museum. This suggests that the motif was copied from the same source, or was passed from one embroiderer to another.
© Embroiderers' Guild.

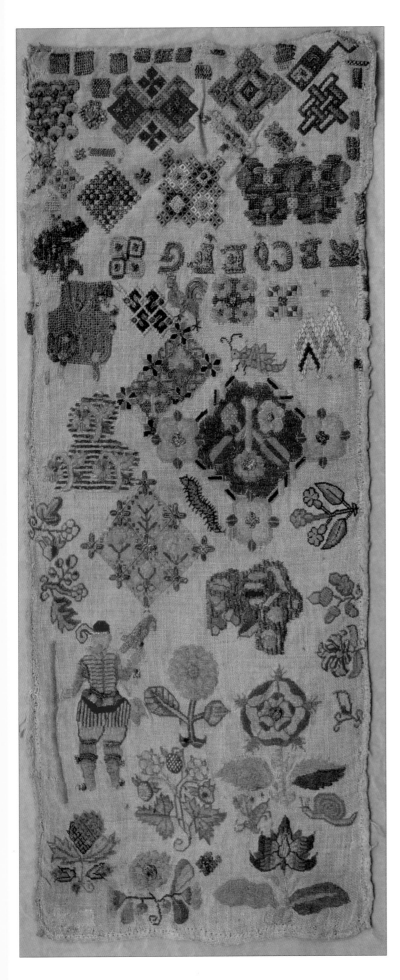

Fig. 53. Detail from the sampler (left).
This example of Elizabethan Celyon stitch
has 4-columns of loops, each making single
connections. The stitching is worked in gilt
passing and is around 5 mm wide.

Fig. 54. Two sections of Elizabethan Ceylon
stitch viewed from the reverse side of the
fabric. They have been worked over the edge
of the fabric so that they enclose the hem.
Both examples are 4-column versions,
though the upper one has a filling of silk
stitches worked over the rungs between each
column. The filling stitches are a form of
back stitch, where the thread works over two
rungs and back underneath one rung
© Embroiderers' Guild.

Among the designs are small blocks of stitching, worked in metallic passing. They form no specific motif, but appear to be just small test pieces of different textures. There are eight examples of Elizabethan Ceylon stitch. They are all constructed from columns with loops forming single connections, though the number of columns varies, as does the type of fillings that have been added onto the rungs between the columns. Five of the examples are illustrated in the photographs.

More information:
Articles in *Embroidery* Vol. 53 (2002) and Vol 54 (2003)

Fig. 55. The front (above) and back (right) of a striped background made from Elizabethan knitting stitch, worked in alternate rows of passing and silk.
© *Embroiderers' Guild.*

  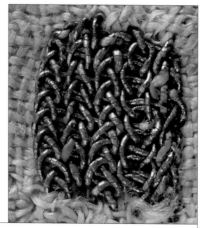

Fig. 56. Three examples of 3-column Elizabethan Ceylon stitch, each with a different filling. They measure around 8 to 9 mm in width. The filling stitches are made from the same passing thread used to make the underlying stitch. The filling stitches are worked over one set of rungs, before turning and working over the second sets of rungs. **Left:** A filling of back stitches that work underneath six rungs and back over three rungs. **Centre:** A filling of back stitches that work underneath three rungs and back over two rungs. **Right:** A filling of crochet chain. © *Embroiderers' Guild.*

CASE STUDY 4

Example:
Elizabethan Ground Stitch (page 28)
Elizabethan Tubular Ceylon (page 116)
Applied Work (page 152 & 156)
Object:
Panel
Location:
Embroiderers' Guild Collection, London
Accession Number:
EG 1987.50

This panel measures approximately 30 x 21 cm (12 x 8 inches), and is made from a piece of plain-weave linen, with around 15 threads per linear centimetre (38 per inch). The embroidered design centres on a figure, with a stringed instrument, sitting within an arched frame. She is worked in tent stitch, and this stitch is also used to create the bases of the large floral motifs, as well as the small hillocks dotted with flowers at the foot of the design. Two vases, made from Elizabethan trellis stitch, have been placed on the hillocks, and two coiling stems, encircling floral motifs, rise up from each vase. The whole design has been given a three-dimensional quality through the use of raised petals and applied materials. Various types of purl have been attached to provide major design aspects, like the coiling stems, as well as smaller touches, such as flower stamens (see Fig.10, page 13). Small pearls have been added as highlights in various places, and an example can be seen in Fig. 9 (page 12). Little glass beads have been used in a similar way, to make the

eyes on four caterpillar-like creatures. Their striped bodies are constructed from Elizabethan tubular Ceylon stitch, with filling stitches worked over the rungs. This punto-in-aria stitching has been couched down afterwards, and additional stitches have been worked into the fabric alongside the body to give the impression of little black legs (see Fig.127, page 117). Another notable indication of realism and attention to detail can be seen on the thistle motifs. Like other examples from this era, the downy thistle heads have been created from a tassel of silk threads. Only the ends of the tassel protrude out from under the stitching to form the flossy fuzz.

The linen is entirely covered with embroidery, and two different backgrounds have been used to fill the spaces between the motifs. Under the arch, a gilt passing thread has been couched down over the linen's surface. The thread zigzags up and down over the ground, with each turn secured at the top and bottom by taking the passing underneath the fabric for a short distance. The main expanse of the passing has been couched down using a separate pink silk thread that has now faded. The

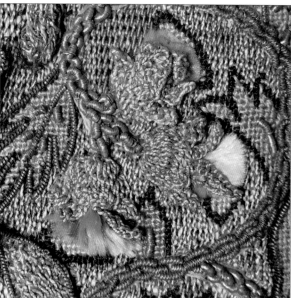

Fig. 57. Detail of the downy thistle heads made from tufts of silk. Note the difference in texture as the coiling stem changes from flat strip (top left) to round wire purl (bottom).
© Embroiderers' Guild.

couching stitches have been carefully placed, so that they each work over two passing threads, and co-ordinated together, with nine couching stitches creating little diamonds. Outside of the arch, the background is made from Elizabethan ground stitch worked in a silver passing thread. There are subtle variations in the size and angle of the stitching as it negotiates its way around the motifs. Generally, the tension is firm so that the linen weave is distorted and pairs of linen threads are pressed together.

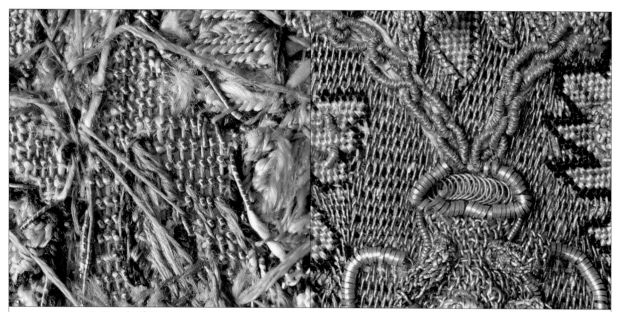

Fig. 58. Details of the panel seen on the opposite page, showing the front and back of Elizabethan ground stitch. The linen fabric is distorted as the stitching squeezes together pairs of linen threads creating gaps in the stitching.
© Embroiderers' Guild.

CASE STUDY 5

Example:
Elizabethan Gobelin Stitch (page 30)
Object:
Book Cover
Location:
British Library, London
Shelfmark:
Davis 63

Areas of Elizabethan Gobelin stitch can seem a little sparse when compared to other background filling stitches, and this might explain why it was seldom found fulfilling this role. However, this example illustrates two ways in which the stitch has been augmented to help add volume to the finished result.

The Booke of Common Prayer and *The Psalter* are bound together in this embroidered cover. Both were printed in London, and are thought to date from 1582. Handwritten on the inside of the front cover is "Dulcebella Phillipps her booke" and further text gives the dates of various events, such as her marriage to Ambrose Phillipps in 1636, the birth dates of their children, and various deaths, including that of King Charles I.

The book's cover portrays a latticework design set on a striking red silk embroidered background, worked onto a plain-weave linen fabric that has approximately 13-15 threads along a centimetre length (33-38 per inch). The lattice framework is bordered with green silk, and filled with several different stitches, including Elizabethan Gobelin. In places, the stitch has been enhanced with the addition of purl. Short lengths have been threaded onto the surface sections of each stitch, so that the purl helps to create a denser filling for the motif. The diameter of the purl compares to a modern size No. 8, but the flattened strip of metal is thicker and wider than the modern counterpart. The coils do not sit in a neat spiral, but are tightly packed together in an erratic muddle.

At first glance the grey and pale green parts of the lattice have an appearance similar to Roumanian stitch (see page 40). However, the worn edges of the cover reveal lines of Elizabethan Gobelin stitch, with the chevron affect created by working alternate lines of S- and Z-slanting stitches. The gaps that appear between each line of silk stitching have been filled in afterwards with a row of back stitches. They are worked

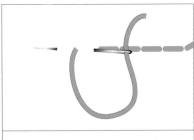

Fig. 59. Modern back stitch.

in the same coloured silk, and make a (0:1) surface section that covers the tips of the Elizabethan Gobelin stitches. The back stitches are illustrated in the diagram with a slant to clarify their path. In reality, the silk did not always fall to the same side of the underneath section and was also seen piercing itself in places.

More information:
An image of the book cover is available on-line in the British Library's database of bookbindings.

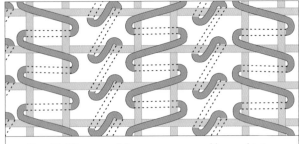

Fig. 60. Diagram of the structure created by combining Elizabethan Gobelin with back stitches. Note that the back stitches are illustrated with a slant just to clarify their path.

CASE STUDY 6

Example:
Elizabethan Plaited Gobelin (page 32)
Applied Work (page 154)
Object:
Panel
Location:
Ashmolean Museum, Oxford
Accession Number:
WA1947.191.306

The embroidered section of this panel measures approximately 38 x 50 cm (15 x 20 inches). It has an internal border, marked out with the remains of black silk tent stitches, measuring around 30 x 40cm (12 x 16 inches). The images outside the black borderline are intriguing, as they include coats of arms and the date 1629. The border also contains two obelisks entwined with plants, a design that can be found in emblem books, and is associated with a symbolic reading of *While you stand, I shall flourish*.

Embroidered panels depicting biblical scenes were popular in the 17th century, and here the central image illustrates the finding of Moses. The surrounding flora and fauna is typical of the period, as each motif sits in relative isolation and is scaled in unrealistic proportions. The background is embroidered in Elizabethan plaited Gobelin stitch worked in a fine metallic passing. It provides a rich contrast to the motifs that are mainly worked in silk tent stitches. Further colouring comes from the partially exposed silk core of elongated passing. Both the flat strip and round wire versions have been used, either couched down flat or rolled into little coils to create a raised texture, which is particularly effective for the mounds of grass. Additional features, such as black beads for eyes and flat plate for the sun's rays (Fig. 160, page 154) also help to enhance the quality of this panel.

More information:
Brooks, M. (2004) *English Embroideries of the Sixteenth and Seventeenth Centuries in the collection of the Ashmolean Museum.*

Fig. 61. Detail of the panel showing the unrealistic scale of a deer and honeysuckle motif. They were worked in silk tent stitch on a background of Elizabethan plaited Gobelin.
© *Ashmolean Museum, University of Oxford.*

CASE STUDY 7

Example:
Elizabethan half stitch (page 34)
Object:
Purse, or Sweet bag
Location:
Gallery of Costume, Platt Hall, Manchester
Accession Number:
1951.441

The term *sweet bag* has been used to describe a particular type of small square purse, such as those seen in this case study and on pages 61, 139 and 149. Nonetheless, it is uncertain as to whether the surviving examples relate to those mentioned in documents from the 16th and 17th century. The name *sweet bag* is thought to derive from the filling of bags with perfumed contents, but there is no specific evidence relating scented goods to this purse, and it is just as likely to have been used as a container for small items, or gifted money.

Although this early 17th century purse is not the most striking example in the Platt Hall collection, it is still of interest. Measuring about 12 cm (approximately 5 inches) square, the plain-weave linen fabric has around 13-15 threads per centimetre (33-38 threads per inch), and is completely covered with stitches. The design is a somewhat disorderly version of coiling stems encircling floral motifs, such as rose, borage and carnation. They are embroidered in tent stitch, worked in different shades of coloured silk. As normal, the motifs are bordered with black, though the dye has disintegrated most of this particular colour. The background is more unusual as it is a combination of trammed Elizabethan half stitches highlighted with back stitches.

Tramming is a term used to describe a technique where extra threads are added underneath needlepoint. The threads are laid parallel to the fabric weave, and are covered by working stitches over the top of them. The background of the Platt Hall purse has been trammed with a silver passing thread that sits between two linen threads. The same metallic thread is turned at the end of the row and used to make the Elizabethan half stitches that cover it. The tramming

thread pads out these stitches and raises them upwards. The lines of Elizabethan half stitch have been further emphasised by adding a row of yellow silk back stitches between each line of trammed work. They are stitched into the spaces already created by the silver passing, thus squeezing the paired linen threads further together and filling in the distorted gaps. The silk has been taken underneath four linen threads (0:4) at the back, and returns over two threads on the surface (0:2). The result is a densely packed background with a slightly raised texture, which all seems a little too complex for the short rows of background that fit between the contours of the floral motifs. Once again in order to clarify the diagram, the back stitches are illustrated at a slant, even though they didn't always conform to this structure.

More information:
An image of thepurse is available on-line in the Gallery of Costume's "Search the collection" database.

> A recipe from *Delightes for Ladies, to adorn their Persons, Tables, Closets, and distillatories,* by K. Platt (1602).
>
> Sweet bags to lie among linnen.
>
> Fill your bags only with lignum Rhodium finely beaten, and it will give an excellent sent to your linnen.

Tramming

Stitching from top-to-bottom

Surface section - Start at A, at the top of the column, and lay the thread parallel to the linen weave, between the threads that will form the column of half stitching. At the base of the column, take the needle 'right 1' and into the fabric at B.

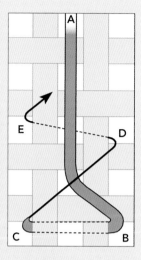

Turning at the bottom of the column

Underneath section - From B, work under the linen weave 'left 2' into C.

Stitching from top-to-bottom

Work a column of Z-slanting Elizabethan half stitch (page 34) covering the AB thread.

Turning at the top of the column

The last stitch is finished partway through the sequence, so that only step one is worked in the usual way. The needle is then taken under the linen 'right 1' to exit the linen. This will be the new position A, ready to start the next column.

Shaping

Only the turn at the top of the column needs to be altered when shaping the background. Here, the underneath section of the stitch may need elongating and angling to reach A, so that this position sits at the top of the column between the two linen threads that will be covered by the subsequent stitching.

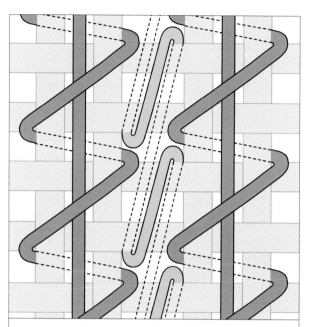

Fig. 62. The structure of the stitching found on the Platt Hall bag. Rows of trammed Elizabethan half stitch have been interspersed with yellow silk back stitches.

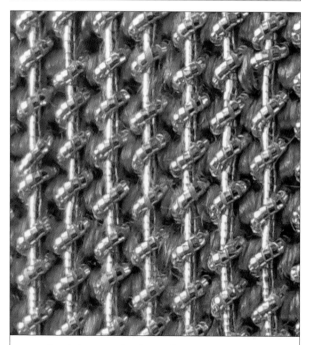

Fig. 63. The raised ridges of trammed Elizabethan half stitch worked in modern passing with yellow silk back stitches.

CASE STUDY 8

Example:
Elizabethan half-and-turn stitch (page 36)
Object:
Book Cover
Location:
British Library, London
Shelfmark:
C.194.a.915

Christopher Barker was an eminent 16th century publisher, and as the book's title page declares, he was "printer to the Queenes most excellent Maiestie" Elizabeth I. He held the patent for publishing the bible and produced this copy of the New Testament in 1586. The book has been encased in an embroidered cover, worked onto a plain-weave linen fabric, which has approximately 10 threads along a centimetre length (25 per inch). The same geometric motif is repeated across the whole cover, worked in either blue or green silk, with an un-dyed thread enhanced with purl adding onto the stitch's surface section. The purl is made from a flat strip of metal, wound in a coil that compares to a modern size No. 8. However, the coils do not sit in a neat spiral, but are squashed tightly together in an erratic muddle. In addition, the flat strip is generally wider and thicker than the modern version, though the size does vary quite dramatically along a length.

The net-like texture of the red background is created from lines of Elizabethan half-and-turn stitch.

Between each line, the red silk thread doubles back, working a row of back stitches that cover (0:2) linen threads on the surface section. These back stitches produce the straight lines that visually complete the 'boxing-in' of the half stitch's diagonal line. They also help to distort the underlying fabric by increasing the gaps between the linen threads. Another outcome is that lines of Elizabethan half-and-turn stitch were worked in the same direction, because the thread then turns to work back stitches in the opposite direction. However, there appeared to be no uniform way of working, as both the S- and Z-slanting versions of Elizabethan half-and-turn stitch were found on this book cover.

More information:
An image of the book cover is available on-line in the British Library's database of bookbindings.

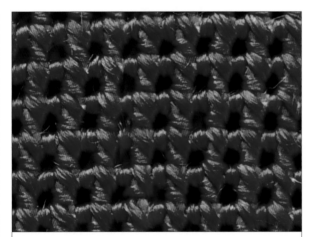

Fig. 64. Sample of the background stitching. The result looks remarkably similar to Elizabethan square net.

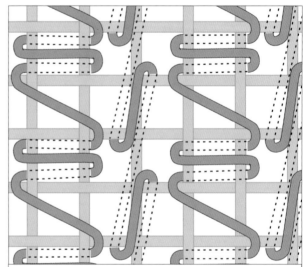

Fig. 65. Diagram illustrating the structure of the background stitching. Note that the back stitches are illustrated with a slant to clarify its path. In reality, the silk did not always fall to the same side of the underneath section and often pierced itself.

CASE STUDY 9

Example:
Elizabethan Square Net (page 38)
Object:
Sampler
Location:
Dorset County Museum, Dorchester
Accession Number:
T903 (1917.8.2)

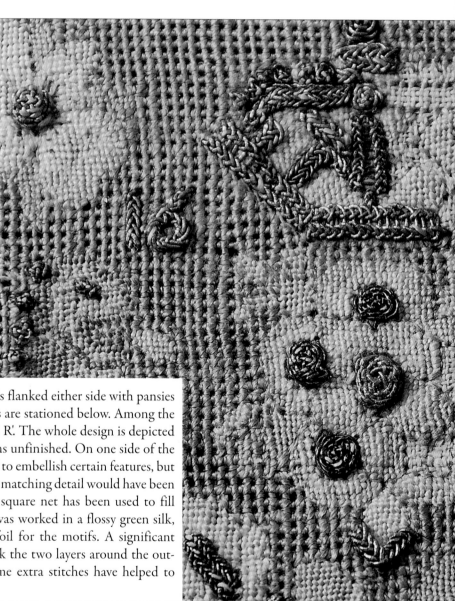

This spot sampler measures around 22cm (8½ inches) wide, and 54cm (21 inches) in height. This is the full loom width of the fabric, because the selvedge, highlighted with a blue warp thread, is visible at both the top and bottom of the sampler. The linen fabric is covered in a wide range of designs that have been inked onto the surface. Although the outlines are clearly marked, many of the motifs are unfinished. Individual motifs include flowers, animals and insects, as well as a man and woman dressed in period costume. There is also a selection of geometric designs.

In the middle of the sampler, there are various royal icons within the confines of a rectangle that measures approximately 12cm wide and 11cm high (roughly 4 inches). At the centre is a Tudor rose topped with a crown. It is flanked either side with pansies and lions, whilst a pair of virile unicorns are stationed below. Among the motifs are the date '1630' and initials 'C R'. The whole design is depicted in detail using silk stitches, but it remains unfinished. On one side of the rectangle, metallic passing has been used to embellish certain features, but the linen fabric is still exposed where the matching detail would have been worked on the other half. Elizabethan square net has been used to fill most of the rectangle's background. It was worked in a flossy green silk, and creates a uniform and restrained foil for the motifs. A significant amount of shaping was required to work the two layers around the outlines of these motifs, and in places some extra stitches have helped to improve the silhouette.

Fig. 66. Detail of the central rectangular design, with a background of Elizabethan square net.
© *The Dorset Natural History and Archaeological Society at the Dorset County Museum.*

CASE STUDY 10

Example:
Elizabethan Roumanian Stitch (page 40)
Object:
Book Cover
Location:
British Library, London
Shelfmark:
C.66.e.10

After Christopher Barker (see page 58) died in 1599, his patents and privileges passed to his son, Robert. When Queen Elizabeth I died in 1603, Robert continued as the royal printer, and is renowned for publishing the King James Bible. However, Robert had financial difficulties, and in 1620 this copy of *The Booke of Common Prayer* was produced in partnership with John Bill.

The book is covered with a rectangle of linen fabric that extends around the whole outer surface, measuring approximately 34 x 20 cm (13 x 8 inches). Two pairs of ties once secured the covers together, though little remains of them today. The plain-weave linen has around 11-12 threads along a centimetre length (28-30 per inch) and is embroidered with a geometric design, bordered top and bottom with a straight line. The design is composed of two interlocking motifs, one worked in green silk and the other in pale pink silk. The same design can be seen on a sampler in the Victoria & Albert Museum (Accession Number T.80-1918).

The motifs are formed from connecting squares, each consisting of four by four linen threads. The motifs are filled with Elizabethan Roumanian stitch, though these are adapted in places to shape the ends of the blocks. The intricacy of the design is enhanced as the stitches are arranged in a regular format, so that the same parts of each motif are always stitched horizontally or vertically. However, the motifs were not worked in an orderly fashion, as the stitches are not always pointing the same way. For example, some of the horizontal 'spurs' on the green motifs are worked in mirror image to one another, whilst others point in the same direction. The outline around each motif has been emphasised afterwards with passing, couched down at each corner turn with silk. Passing has also been used to add a single Elizabethan spider's web (page 136) at the centre of every pink motif.

More information:
An image of the book cover is available on-line in the British Library's database of bookbindings.

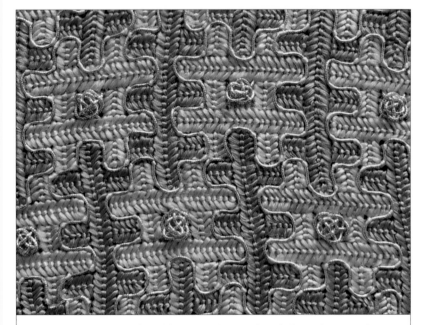

Fig. 67. The design formed from interlocking motifs, worked in modern materials.

CASE STUDY 11

Example:
Elizabethan French Stitch(page 42)
Elizabethan plaited braid stitch - standard (page 68)
Object:
Purse, or Sweet Bag
Location:
Victoria & Albert Museum, London
Accession Number:
T.204-1928

This small purse measures approximately 11 cm square (4 inches), and is thought to date from the mid 17th century. Its construction corresponds to those described as sweet bags (see page 56). It is made from a rectangle of linen folded in half and seamed up the two sides. Three small tassels adorn the base of the purse, and two gimp features have been added at the top corners. Although broken, a silk and passing braid handle is still in situ. However, the matching drawstrings are missing, though evidence of their existence can be seen in the sixteen holes that remain around the top opening of the purse. The pink silk grosgrain lining is also partially missing, but this loss is our gain as it allows a clear view of the reverse side of the embroidery.

The entire purse is covered with Elizabethan French stitch, worked in a flossy silk that spreads well over the linen weave, which has around 16 threads per linear centimetre. The construction of Elizabethan French stitch lends itself to making diagonal lines, and here the design is ideally suited for this stitch. The geometric design comprises a green latticework sitting on a contrasting red background. Each lozenge contains a central motif embroidered in pale blue, brown and cream silk, highlighted in the corners with metallic passing thread. The passing is worked in very short sections of standard Elizabethan plaited braid stitch that fills the space where two Elizabethan French stitches would fit. The versatile embroiderer has worked the Elizabethan French stitch at different slants as they filled in the areas with coloured silk.

Fig. 68. A modern copy of the design on the sweet bag.

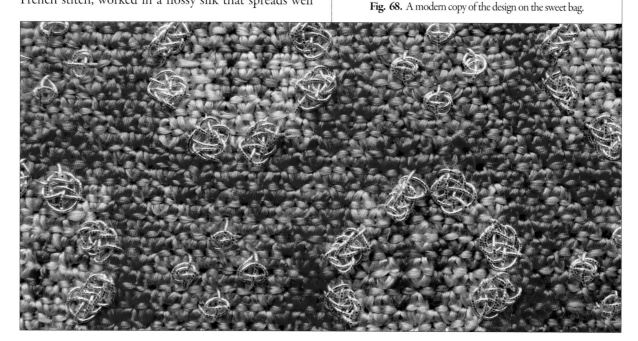

61

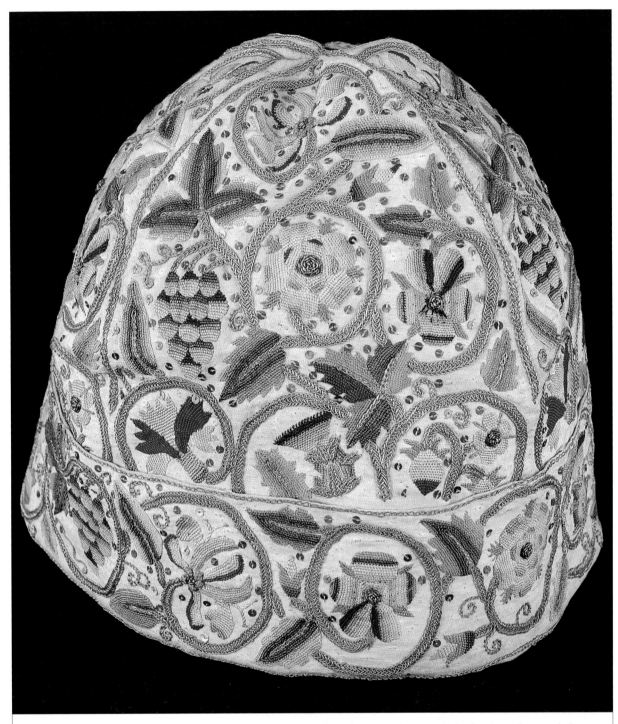

Fig. 69. A gentleman's cap, dating from the early 17th century. The coiling stems that encircle the floral motifs are made from standard Elizabethan plaited braid stitch worked in gilt passing.
© *Witney Antiques.*

Braid stitches

There is no specific terminology for the following selection of stitches, so they have been grouped together as 'braid' stitches, as this seems a unifying term. The stitches are related in that for every stitch the thread forms the shape of an overhand knot. Only a small section of each stitch is worked underneath the fabric. Yet on the surface of the fabric, the thread is taken back under and over itself to form more complex stitching.

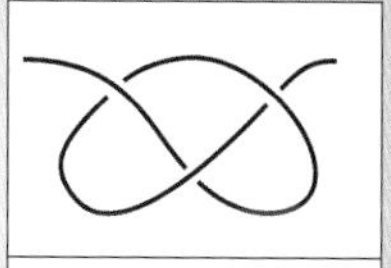

The terms *exit* and *entry* points will be used throughout this section. These will help to identify the points at which the needle exits the fabric (working from underneath to the surface), and where it enters the fabric (going from the surface to underneath the fabric). These points control the stitch's size and evenness. They are usually arranged in parallel lines, with the width of each stitch controlled by the distance between the lines, and the density regulated by the gap between each pair of points (Fig. 71). It is possible to work uniform stitches by using the linen grid as a guide. However, the historic versions were usually worked in a flowing freeform manner, even when they were used in conjunction with needlepoint. You will find that there is an optimum arrangement for different thread sizes, so test each new thread to get a feel for the spacing. This is in keeping with period practise, as you will often see little test pieces on surviving items. The stitches in this section were usually found worked in metallic passing, and the robust thread tends to sit in natural curves. However, apply minimum tension to your stitching action to help keep the stitch structure firm but open.

Fig. 70.
An overhand knot.

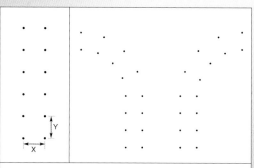

Fig. 71. The entry and exit points are arranged in parallel lines. The distance 'x' controls the width of the stitching, whilst 'y' alters the density. Shaping the stitches is achieved by adding a curve to the parallel lines.

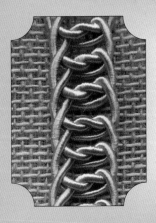

Elizabethan Ladder braid stitch

Elizabethan ladder braid stitch creates a dense ladder-like effect with the rungs appearing as alternate textures: a straight sunken line and a raised twisted bar. The density of the stitch is controlled as the needle enters the fabric. The entry points need to be sufficiently spaced to allow for the needle to pass back through the stitching when creating the straight line (made in step two) in subsequent stitches.

The methods shown in this section all involve the needle being taken under and over the surface sections of previous stitching. Historic examples were found worked in metallic passing, and the firmness of this thread helps to hold open the structure, and to allow the needle to pass easily between sections. The method shown here for reproducing Elizabethan ladder braid follows this theme. However, examples were also found worked in silk, and for this material step one would not be ideal as the needle is more likely to 'pierce' the multiple fibres. The alternative action (Fig. 73) offers a better option for this material. It can also be used for metallic passing, though be aware that the action can be a little more abrasive. Whichever route is taken, the tensioning of the first two steps of the stitch has a tendency to straighten the thread, and lift the end of the previous stitch. This makes a more pronounced slant as the latter part of the stitching is lifted, and was observed in some of the original work.

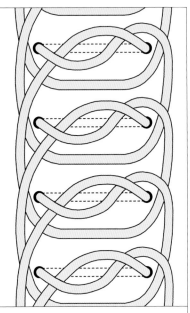

Fig. 72. Structure of Elizabethan ladder braid stitch.

An example of Elizabethan ladder braid stitch is illustrated in Case Study 12 (page 76) and Case Study 13 (page 84).

A start

Bring the needle to the surface at position A. Take the needle over the fabric and enter the fabric at B, above and to the right of the exit point A. Then bring the needle underneath the fabric in a straight line from right-to-left, to exit the fabric at C.

Take the needle down over the thread AB, and bring the needle underneath this thread section, from bottom-to-top. Take the needle round to the right, and go into the fabric at D, beneath entry point B.

Take the needle underneath the fabric in a straight line from right-to-left, and exit the fabric at E, close to position A.

Bring the needle up to the right and enter the fabric at F, directly above entry point B. Take the needle underneath the fabric in a straight line from right-to-left, and exit the fabric at G, ready to start working normally.

Stitching bottom-to-top

Step One:

Surface section - Bring the needle down over the previous stitch. Slide the needle underneath the thread forming the last surface section of the previous stitch. Make sure the needle goes underneath this thread from bottom-to-top. This makes the raised twisted 'rung'.

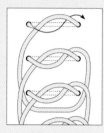

Step Two:

Surface section - Bring the needle down along the right edge, to a position where there are two entry points above it. Angle the needle perpendicular to the stitching, and take it under three sections of thread (one on the right and two on the left-hand side). This makes the straight line 'rung'.

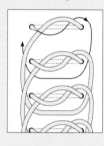

Step Three:

Surface section - Bring the needle up above the stitching, arcing from left-to-right, and enter the fabric a little above of the previous entry point. Make sure there is sufficient space for the subsequent straight line made in step two. Do not tension this thread too tightly, as it will need to have a little 'give' for the subsequent twist made in step one.

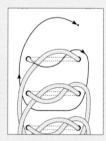

Step Four:

Underneath section - Take the needle underneath the fabric in a straight line from right-to-left, and exit the fabric directly above the previous exit point.

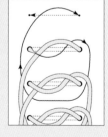

Continue repeating the four steps.

A finish

Complete step two, then bring the needle up above the stitching and enter the fabric on the left-hand side. Secure the thread underneath the fabric.

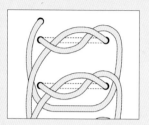

Shaping

Straight lines are achieved by working the exit and entry points in straight parallel lines. To curve the stitching to the left, take the needle into the fabric (in this instance, step three) slightly higher than usual, and to the left of the previous entry point. In addition, angle the underneath section (in this instance, step four slightly downward, so that the needle exits a little closer than usual, and more to the left of the previous exit point (see Fig. 71 for the path of exit/entry points).

To curve the stitching to the right, make the same adjustments but to the right rather left.

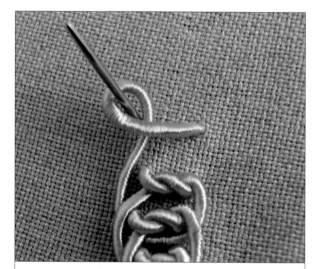

Fig. 73. An alterative action for step one. As the needle exits the fabric at the beginning of step one, wind an anti-clockwise loop of thread around the tip of the needle. Continue with the other three steps, though note that you will need to leave the thread slack at the end of step three, so that there is sufficient thread to wrap around the needle. Pull any surplus thread through after step one.

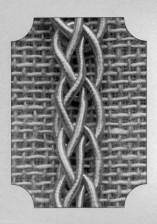

Elizabethan holly braid stitch

It is not easy to choose a name for an obsolete stitch. The term *holly* was used to temporarily identify this stitch when the author first discovered it on an object dubbed the 'holly coif' (see page 84). However, the term has since become ingrained, as no other suitable term has been suggested.

The visual appearance of Elizabethan holly braid stitch resembles a three-ridged twill braid. It is related to the plaited braid stitches (pages 68-75), as all of their structures are built from the same component. Each stitch section above the surface of the fabric forms an overhand knot shape around the entry/exit points. The stitching varies depending on how these shapes are joined together. The plaited braid versions all connect the shapes together in a vertical plane, but Elizabethan holly braid stitch links the shape sideways. This alters both the appearance of the stitch and the rhythm of movement used to create it. Unlike all the other stitches in this group, the thread underneath the fabric does not form a series of parallel dashes (see Fig. 75). Instead, a line of S-slanting dashes is formed. The entry and exit points are usually set close together, and can also be positioned with the exit point sitting directly above the entry point. In these instances, the narrow close-set stitching will produce a straight line of dashes on the reverse of the fabric.

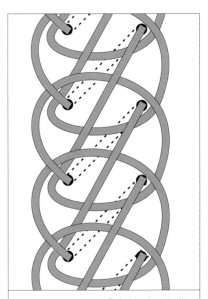

Fig. 74. Structure of Elizabethan holly braid stitch

An example of Elizabethan holly braid stitch is illustrated in Case Study 12 (page 66) and Case Study 13 (page 84).

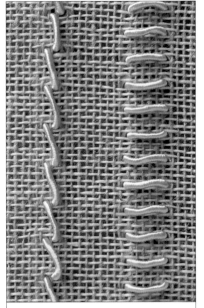

Fig. 75. Elizabethan holly braid stitch (left) creates a line of dashes at the back of the fabric, compared to the parallel dashes formed by the Elizabethan plaited braid stitches (right).

Tensioning Tip.

Tighten the stitch after step two, by taking the needle to the upper left and drawing the thread up until the desired arch is created (see image below). At step three, do not pull too tightly and keep the thread to the right, so that you can see the exit point in step four.

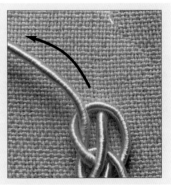

A start

Bring the needle to the surface at exit point A. Enter the fabric at B, above and slightly to the right of the exit point. Take the needle back down underneath the fabric, to the left of A and bring the needle to the surface of the fabric at exit point C.

Bring the needle upwards and to the right, so that the thread forms an arch above position B, and enter the fabric at D. Note that D sits opposite C, with A in between them. Take the needle underneath the fabric to exit at E, within the arch of thread on the surface. Bring the needle up to the right, going over the arch of thread, and enter the fabric at F.

Take the needle underneath the fabric, back down towards the start of the stitching. Exit at G, within the arch of thread on the surface of the fabric, but above position E. You are now ready to start working normally. For the first stitch the needle will lay horizontally just below B, and between E and G.

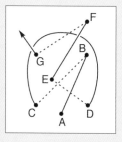

Stitching bottom-to-top

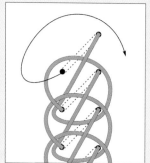

Step One:
Surface section - bring the thread up and to the right forming an arch above the previous stitching.

Step Two:
Surface section - Bring the needle down along the right-hand side, so that the tip is below two previous entry points. Angle the needle perpendicular to the stitching, and take it from right-to-left under the previous stitching and through the arch made in step one. Note that the needle will pass under four threads from the previous stitching (two Z-slanting sections and both edge sections), and through the arch by going under the section closest to the exit hole before crossing over the arch on the left.

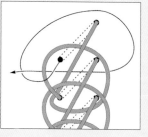

Step Three:
Surface section - take the needle up to the right and enter the fabric directly above the previous entry point.

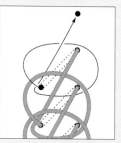

Step Four:
Underneath section - Take the needle under the fabric and downwards to exit the fabric within the arch of thread, making sure that it is above the thread descending into the entry point.

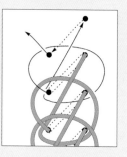

A finish

At step three, enter the fabric in a central position, just above the stitching. Secure the thread underneath the fabric.

Shaping

To curve the stitching to the left, enter and exit the fabric more to the left than you would normally. To curve the stitching to the right, enter the fabric more to the right than you would normally.

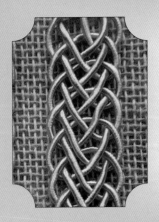

Elizabethan plaited braid stitch (standard)

This version of Elizabethan plaited braid stitch has been selected as the 'standard' because it appeared to be the most popular, having been found on many surviving items. Typically, it was seen forming the coiling stems around floral motifs, though it was also found making geometric designs, and acting as a covering over seams.

The historic stitch resembles a flat four-ridge twill braid, and is usually identified as the modern version of plaited braid stitch (see Fig 77) Indeed, this attribution is applied to all the variations of the historic stitch. However, there are structural differences between the modern and Elizabethan versions. These are best examined by starting at one end of the thread as it exits the fabric, and then observing the number of threads it travels under and over before it enters back into the fabric (see Fig. 83, page 73). Nonetheless, the biggest difference between the modern and Elizabethan stitches can be found by examining the direction in which they are worked (see Fig. 78). The modern method is worked back-to-front, starting where the historic version would end, and finishing where the other would start. Working in this manner has given modern plaited braid stitch

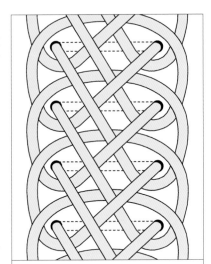

Fig. 76. Structure created by standard Elizabethan plaited braid stitch.

a reputation for difficulty. Thankfully, the Elizabethan version is easier to produce. In addition to starting the stitch at the opposite end to the modern way, practical experiment has found that positioning the stitches so that they are worked in a bottom-to-top direction helped to create a comfortable angle for the needle.

The working method for all the plaited braid stitches is based on the same four actions. They are best worked in metallic passing, as the robust thread will form a natural curve when arched above the stitching (in step two). The stitches can be worked relatively loosely, as these firm threads will hold their shape. Indeed, tight stitching can hinder the needle as it passes back through the previous stitching in steps one and three. It is small changes in these two steps that alter the number of threads that the needle passes under and over. These differences modify the density and appearance of each variation. To help highlight the differences in the two steps, each variation will be summarised in the same manner. The standard version can be summed up in the following way:

Over 1, under 3. Arch.
Under 3, over 2. Underneath.

An example of standard Elizabethan plaited braid stitch is illustrated in Case Study 11 (page 61) and Case Study 14 (page 86).

Fig. 77. Modern plaited braid stitch.

Fig. 78. Diagram showing the route of Elizabethan plaited braid stitch, which starts at A and loops round to enter the fabric at B. In contrast, the modern version creates the same loop shape, but starts at B and finishes by entering the fabric at A.

A start

Secure the thread under the fabric, and bring the needle to the surface at exit point A. Take the needle upwards and enter the fabric at B, above and to the left of exit point A.

Take the needle underneath the fabric in a straight line from left-to-right, and exit the fabric at C. Take the needle under the thread section AB, going from right-to-left. Bring the needle upwards and to the right so that the thread forms an arch above the stitching.

Take the needle upwards and to the left going under the thread that exits at C, and over the arch you have just made. Enter the fabric at D.

Take the needle underneath the fabric in a straight line from left-to-right and exit the fabric at E, ready to start working normally.

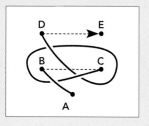

Stitching bottom-to-top

Step One:
Surface section - Take the needle at an angle through the previous stitching, from top-right to bottom-left, going over the first thread (an arch) and under another three threads (two S-slanting sections and an edge section). Note there are two entry points above the slant of the needle.

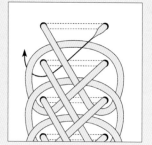

Step Two:
Surface section - Bring the thread up over the stitching, from left-to-right, to form an arch shape.

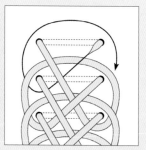

Step Three:
Surface section - Bring the needle down along the right-hand side, so that the tip is below two previous exit points. Take the needle at an angle through the previous stitching, from bottom-right to top-left, going under three threads (an edge and two Z-slanting sections) and over the two arched threads (one of these is the arch made in step two). Enter the fabric directly above the previous entry point.

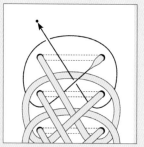

Step Four:
Underneath section - Take the needle underneath the fabric in a straight line from left-to-right and exit the fabric directly above the previous exit point. Continue repeating the four steps.

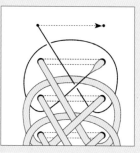

Shaping

Straight lines are achieved by working the exit and entry points in straight parallel lines. To curve the stitching to the left, take the needle into the fabric (in this instance step three) slightly lower than usual, and to the left of the previous entry point. In addition, angle the underneath section (in this instance step four) slightly upwards, so that the needle exits a little higher than usual, and more to the left of the previous exit point (Fig. 71, page 63).

To curve the stitching to the right, make the same adjustments but to the right rather left.

A finish

At step three, enter the fabric in a more central position, just above the stitching. Secure the thread underneath the fabric.

Elizabethan plaited braid stitch (variation one)

O f the plaited braid variations, this version appeared the most frequently on examined items. It is worked in the same way as the standard stitch except that more threads are worked through in step one, resulting in a denser, more complex structure. It takes a little while to set up the start, as sufficient sections need to be in place before normal working practice can commence. The working action can be summarised as the following:

Over 2, under 4. Arch.

Under 3, over 2. Underneath.

An example of Elizabethan plaited braid stitch (variation one) is illustrated in Case Study 15 (page 92) and Case Study 22 (page 144).

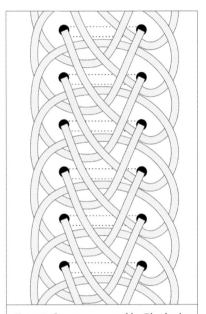

Fig. 79. Structure created by Elizabethan plaited braid stitch (variation one).

Fig. 80. Steps one and three showing the needle passing through the previous stitching at an angle.

A finish

At step three, enter the fabric in a more central position, just above the stitching. Secure the thread underneath the fabric.

Shaping

As described for Elizabethan plaited braid stitch (page 69).

A start

Secure the thread underneath the fabric and exit to the surface at A. Bring the thread up and to the right, forming a loose arch shape and take the needle into the fabric at B. Take the needle underneath the fabric from right-to-left and exit the fabric at C, halfway between A and B.
Bring the needle up to the left, over the arch of thread, and take the needle into the fabric at D. Take the needle underneath the fabric from left-to-right and exit at E.

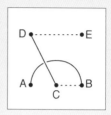

From E, take the needle down and to the left, going over one (the arch) and under two threads (CD and the left-hand part of the arch). Bring the thread up and to the right, forming a new arch above the stitching. Enter the fabric at F, close to entry point B. Take the needle underneath the fabric to exit at G, between the arch AB and the start of the thread coming out of E. Bring the needle up to the left, over two threads (both arches) and enter the fabric at H. Take the needle underneath the fabric from left-to-right and exit the fabric at I. You are now ready to start working normally.
Note that the first stitch will pass under GH, CD, and under th left-hand curved sections of AB and EF.

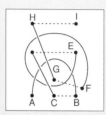

Stitching bottom-to-top

Step One:
Surface section - Take the needle at an angle through the previous stitching, from top-right to bottom-left, going over two threads (both arches) and under four threads (two S-slanting threads and two edge threads). Note there are two entry points above the slant of the needle.

Step Two:
Surface section - Bring the needle up over the stitching from left-to-right, to form an arch shape.

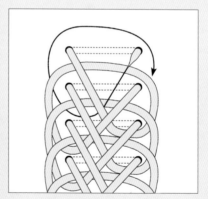

Step Three:
Surface section - Bring the needle down along the right-hand side, so that the tip is below two previous exit points. Take the needle at an angle through the previous stitching, from bottom-right to top-left, going under three threads (an edge and two Z-slanting sections) and over the two arched threads (one of these is the arch made in step two). Enter the fabric directly above the previous entry point.

Step Four:
Underneath section - Take the needle underneath the fabric in a straight line from left-to-right and exit the fabric directly above the previous exit point.
Continue repeating the four steps.

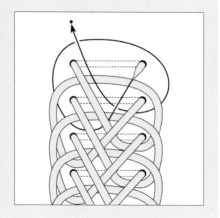

Elizabethan plaited braid stitch (variation two)

This is another denser version of the standard Elizabethan plaited braid stitch, as can be seen by comparing the arch sections of each variation. Variation two has five S- and Z-slanting sections going over it, whilst variation one is crossed by four, and the standard stitch only three (see Fig. 82). Although the structure is more symmetric than variation one, fewer examples were found. As with the previous stitch, more threads are worked through than the standard version, but here it happens in both steps one and three. The path of the needle through the stitching should flow in a single straight line. You may need to adjust the spacing between the exit and entry points in order to get the stitching at an angle where the needle passes through smoothly.

All the plaited braid stitches have the potential to become distorted, especially if the stitching is loose. When this occurs, the metallic threads move around within the stitch structure, altering its visual appearance. It seemed to be a noticeable factor for this stitch, perhaps because of the complexity of the under-and-over structure, and the way that the thread pulls on the arches at the end of step three.

The working method can be summarised by the following:

Over 2, under 4. Arch.

Under 4, over 3. Underneath.

An example of Elizabethan plaited braid stitch (variation two) is illustrated in Case Study 16 (page 94).

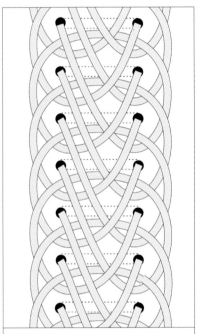

Fig. 81. Structure created by Elizabethan plaited braid stitch (variation two)

A finish

As described for standard Elizabethan plaited braid stitch (page 69).

Shaping

As described for standard Elizabethan plaited braid stitch (page 69).

A start

You can use the same start as shown for Elizabethan plaited braid stitch variation one (page 71).

Stitching bottom-to-top

Step One:
Take the needle at an angle through the previous stitching, from top right to bottom left, going over two threads (both arches) and under four threads (two S-slanting threads and two edge threads).

Step Two:
Bring the needle up over the stitching, from left to right, to form an arch shape.

Step Three:
Bring the needle down along the right-hand side, so that the tip is below two previous exit points and angle the needle from bottom right to top left. Take the needle through the previous stitching going under four threads (two edge threads and two Z-slanting threads) and over three arched threads (one of these is the arch made in step two). Enter the fabric a little in front of the previous stitch.

Step Four:
Take the needle underneath the fabric from left to right and exit the fabric bringing the needle to the surface. Continue repeating the four steps.

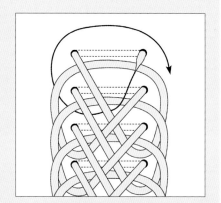

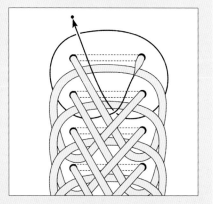

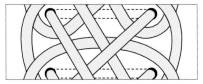

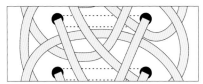

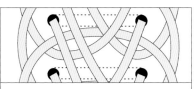

Fig. 82. Comparison of the Elizabethan plaited braid stitches, showing the increasing number of threads that cross the arched section of the stitch.
Top: standard with three
Centre: Variation one with four
Bottom: Variation two with five.

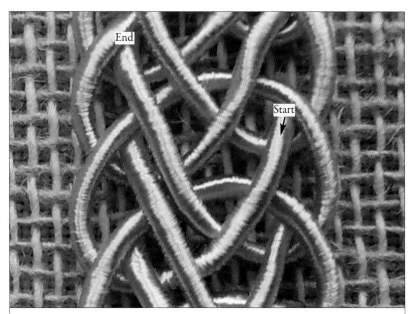

Fig. 83. Examining the structure of standard Elizabethan plaited braid stitch by following the path of a surface stitch section. The thread comes out of the fabric and goes over three, and under three thread sections before arching over two (one is the entry point), under three and over two (one is the exit point). The thread turns again and finally goes under three and over four thread sections.

Elizabethan plaited braid stitch (Cherry variation)

This variation has been referred to as the 'Cherry' variation simply because of the author's first encounter with the stitch on the manuscript 'Cherry 36' (see Case Study 17). This version is simpler and less dense than the standard version of Elizabethan plaited braid stitch, and the other variations shown in this book. The finished stitch still retains the shape of an overhand knot, but unlike the others it only sits around three entry/exit holes. The difference can be seen by comparing Fig. 85 with Fig. 78 on page 68. The working action can be summarised as the following:

Over 1, under 2. Arch.

Under 3, over 2. Underneath.

An example of Elizabethan plaited braid stitch (Cherry variation) is illustrated in Case Study 17 (page 96).

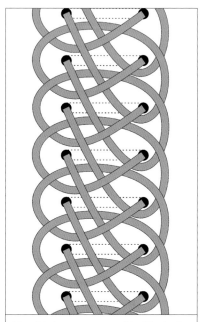

Fig. 84. Structure created by Elizabethan plaited braid stitch (Cherry variation).

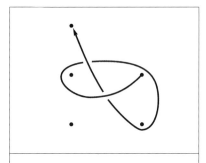

Fig. 85. Here, the thread only travels around three entry/exit points.

A start

As described for standard Elizabethan plaited braid stitch (page 69).

A finish

As described for standard Elizabethan plaited braid stitch (page 69).

Shaping

As described for standard Elizabethan plaited braid stitch (page 69).

Stitching bottom-to-top

Step One:
Take the needle at an angle through the previous stitching, from top right to bottom left, going over one thread (an arch) and under two threads (one S-slanting thread and an edge thread). Note that there is only one entry hole above the needle.

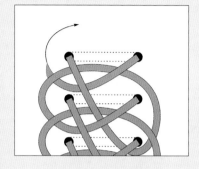

Step Two:
Bring the needle up over the stitching, from left to right, to form an arch shape.

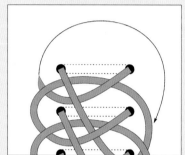

Step Three:
Bring the needle down along the right-hand side, so that the tip is below two previous exit points and angle the needle from bottom right to top left. Take the needle through the previous stitching going under three threads (an edge thread and two Z-slanting threads) and over two arches threads (one of these is the arch made in step two). Enter the fabric a little in front of the previous stitch.

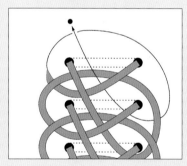

Step Four:
Take the needle underneath the fabric from left to right and exit the fabric bringing the needle to the surface.
Continue repeating the four steps.

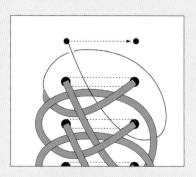

CASE STUDY 12

Example:
Elizabethan Ladder Braid Stitch (page 64)
Elizabethan Holly Braid Stitch (page 66)
Elizabethan Looped Edging (page 102)
Elizabethan Lark's Head Ladder (page 124)
Object:
Fragment
Location:
Private collection

The high value of historic textiles meant that they were often altered and reused. This particular fragment is one of a matching pair, and is thought to be part of a sleeve. Another similar piece of embroidery has also survived, and it is possible that the three fragments are leftover sections from an altered jacket. Each piece is embroidered with silk and metallic passing threads onto a fine linen fabric with around 39 threads per linear centimetre (99 per inch). This segment measures approximately 18 cm (7 inches) along the top edge, 25 cm (10 inches) along the base, and 16 and 12 cm (6 and 5 inches) down the two sides. The longer of the two side edges has been cut, slicing through the embroidery, though there is little evidence of fraying. The other three edges are hemmed, and have an inked border marking the boundary of the stitching. Along the top and shorter side edge, the inked border has been covered in chain stitches (Fig. 111, page 102), worked in gilt passing. The design of coiling stems encircling floral motifs depicts honeysuckle, acorns, grapes and rose. The background is festooned with spangles, each held in place by three stitches worked in a striking red silk.

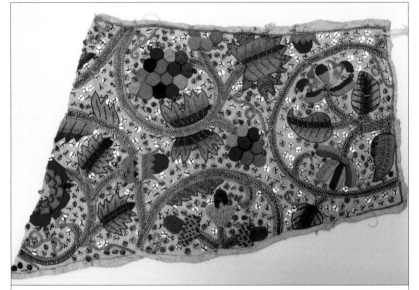

Fig. 86. One of three embroidered fragments, thought to be part of a jacket. Due to limited exposure to light, and a lack of wear and tear, the fragments have retained their vivid colours, giving us a sense of the impact that the embroidery would have made.
© Privately owned. Copyright in the image reserved to the owner.

Although the design on this fragment is mirrored on its matching partner, there are differences in the stitching. It appears that several different stitches were tested in situ before a decision was made that continued throughout the rest of the project. This phenomenon was seen on many other surviving items, though often these test sections are barely noticeable among the colourful profusion of stitches. Here on this fragment, the embroiderer has explored six different ways of interpreting the coiling stems. The first experiment takes place nearest the shortest side seam, and forms the dense stitching of the honeysuckle stalk and the stem that surrounds it. After a brief attempt at two options, the work settles into a tightly packed version of Elizabethan lark's head ladder, worked in gilt passing, with a filling of silver passing wrapped around the rungs. The stitching is approximately 4 mm wide, with around 7 stitches per centimetre (18 per inch). One could speculate that at this point the embroiderer was somewhat daunted by the prospect of continuing with this intense and time-consuming stitch, because the following coiling stem around the acorns takes a much more relaxed approach. This stem is outlined with a line of chain stitches worked in gilt passing. These stitches have been augmented with Elizabethan looped edging, worked in the same material. The edging has been added onto the interior edge of the stem's outline, so that it sits closest to the stitching filling the centre of the stem. Here, the stitches have been worked in a contrasting silver passing threads. At first the embroiderer tried filling the space with zigzag coral stitch, but after a short distance, switched to Elizabethan holly braid stitch, before finally settling down to Elizabethan ladder braid. It seems that the embroiderer was satisfied with the effective balance between scale, texture and ease of production, because the rest of the stems on all of the fragments continue with this arrangement.

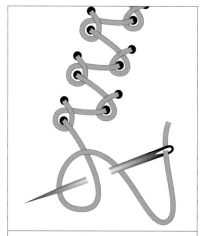

Fig. 87. Modern zigzag coral stitch

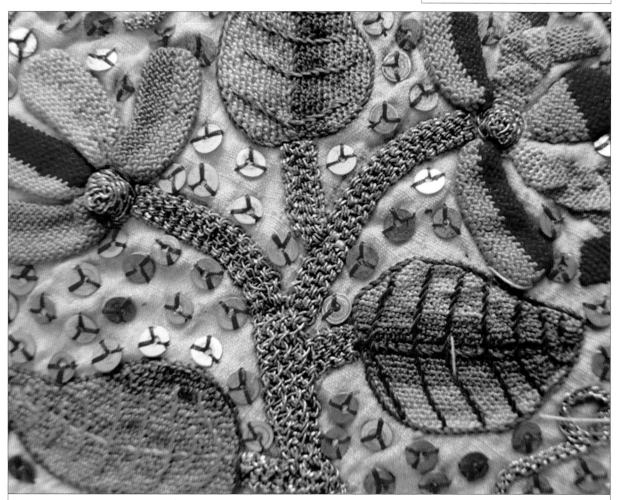

Fig. 88. The embroiderer tried out two different options on the honeysuckle stems, before settling on the Elizabethan lark's head ladder worked in gilt passing, with a dense filling stitch worked in silver passing.
© Privately owned. Copyright in the image reserved to the owner.

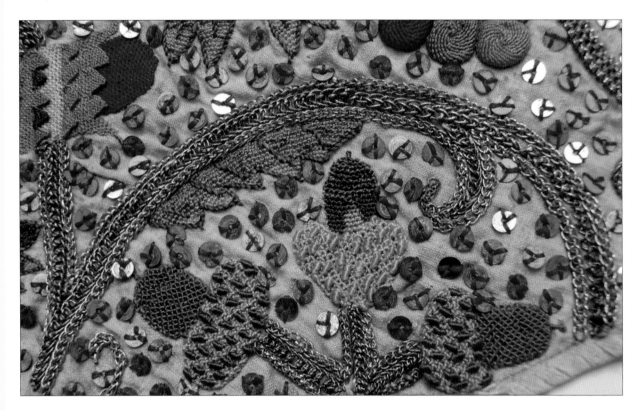

Fig. 89. Front and back of the coiling stem surrounding the acorns. Three more stitches have been tested in the space between the two outlines worked in gilt passing. The right-hand end of the arch starts with zigzag coral stitch, then changes to Elizabethan holly braid stitch, before settling down to Elizabethan ladder braid stitch. A close-up of the back can be seen in Fig. 5, page 8.

© Privately owned. Copyright in the image reserved to the owner.

Fig. 90. Detail of the final choice, which was used for the rest of the coiling stems: Elizabethan ladder braid stitch, bordered by Elizabethan looped edging on chain stitches. The stem averages around 6 mm in width, and has approximately 7 stitches along a centimetre length (18 per inch).

© *Privately owned. Copyright in the image reserved to the owner.*

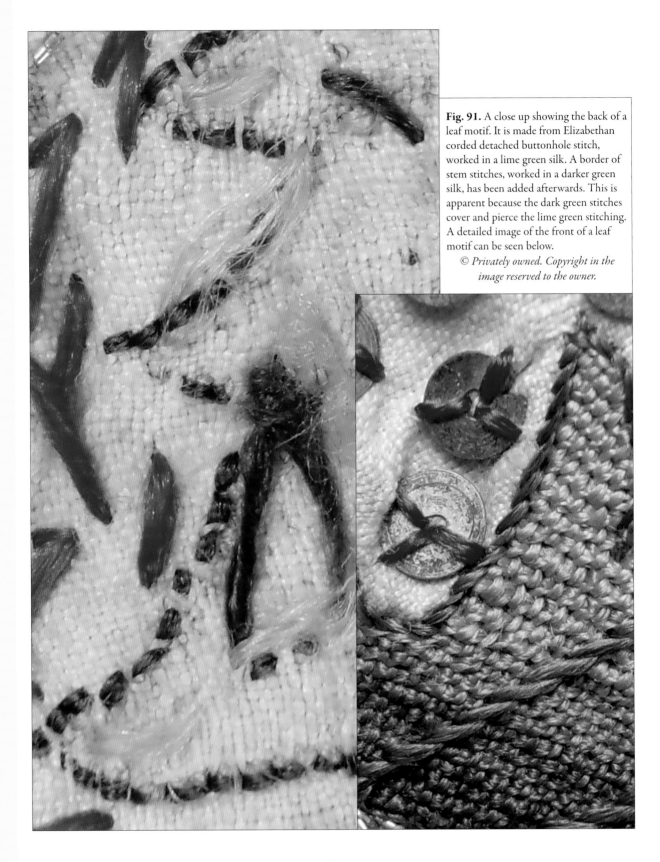

Fig. 91. A close up showing the back of a leaf motif. It is made from Elizabethan corded detached buttonhole stitch, worked in a lime green silk. A border of stem stitches, worked in a darker green silk, has been added afterwards. This is apparent because the dark green stitches cover and pierce the lime green stitching. A detailed image of the front of a leaf motif can be seen below.

© *Privately owned. Copyright in the image reserved to the owner.*

The coiling stems encircle floral motifs, many of which are made using Elizabethan corded detached buttonhole. Some of these petals tips lift off the fabric to become Elizabethan corded Brussels. The fine silk stitches are worked in a flossy thread compromising three strands of loosely S-twisted 2-ply. Sometimes the strands are different hues, creating a variegated blend of colour. The stitches vary in size. Generally there are around 12 loops along a centimetre length (30 per inch), with 17 rows of loops a centimetre (43 per inch), though the stitching is tighter in places.

The edges of the motifs vary, and many have borders added after the main stitching has been completed. For instance, the outline and veins of the leaves have been created from stem stitches (Fig. 30, page 28) added afterwards. The order of stitching is evident as the green silk used for the stem stitches can be seen covering and piercing the edge stitches of the Elizabethan corded detached buttonhole. Some of the Elizabethan corded Brussels has also been edged with Elizabethan looped edging worked in red silk to highlight the rose petals.

Fig. 92. Rose petals of Elizabethan corded detached buttonhole, lifting off into Elizabethan corded Brussels. The petals have been highlighted afterwards with an Elizabethan looped edging worked in red silk.
© *Privately owned. Copyright in the image reserved to the owner.*

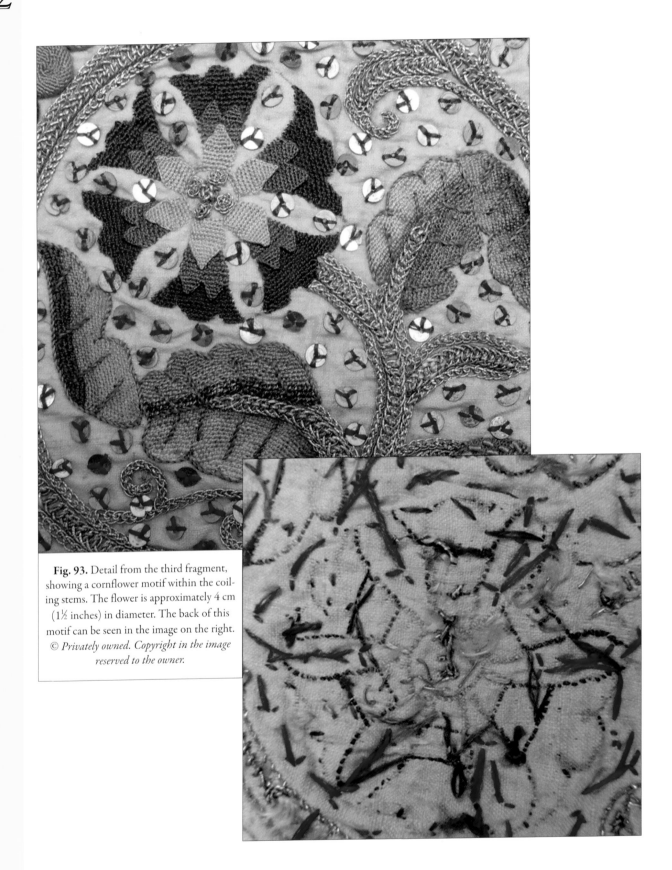

Fig. 93. Detail from the third fragment, showing a cornflower motif within the coiling stems. The flower is approximately 4 cm (1½ inches) in diameter. The back of this motif can be seen in the image on the right.
© *Privately owned. Copyright in the image reserved to the owner.*

Fig. 94. A close up showing the embroidery stitches lifting off the fabric to be worked punto in aria (stitches in air). After the purple and blue sections were completed, a circle of pale blue chain stitches was made at the centre of the flower. The first row of the pale blue Elizabethan corded detached buttonhole stitch was worked into the fabric, over the edge of the chain stitch circle, and then continued outwards from the centre. At first the silk thread was taken into the fabric at the edges. However, after six or seven repeats, the turns are made in midair, and the rows are gradually decreased to make a three-dimensional point. There is no evidence of a cordonet, though the turns give the impression of a slightly raised edge. When the tip of the petal was reached, the working thread was then stitched over the right-hand edge of the point until it reached the fabric, where it was taken underneath the surface. It emerges at the bottom right-hand corner of the completed petal, ready to start working the next clockwise petal.

CASE STUDY 13

Example:
Elizabethan Holly Braid Stitch (page 66)
Elizabethan Ladder Braid Stitch (page 64)
Object:
Coif
Location:
Embroiderers' Guild Collection, London
Accession Number:
EG 162

At some point in its life, someone has sliced into this early 17th century embroidery, leaving it fragmented and with several sections missing. However, sufficient material remains for it to provide a clear understanding of its original form and purpose. In his article for the *Embroidery* magazine, John L Nevinson states that the coif was altered in the 18th century, when the fabric was reused and trimmed with pink ribbon to make sleeves for a baby's garment. The plain-weave linen fabric has around 29 threads per linear centimetre (74 per inch), and was initially cut to shape so that the fabric measured roughly 24 cm (9½ inches) in height, with a minimum width of 39 cm (15 inches), extending to around 46 cm (18 inches).

Originally, the fabric would have been folded in half and stitched together to make a woman's coif similar to the one seen in Case Study 14 (page 86) and Case Study 22 (page 145).

A repeated design extends across the whole coif, though as usual there are inconsistencies, such as in the stitching used to fill the leaves, and in the place-

> **Fig. 95. Below:** The embroidered fragments that once formed an early 17th century coif. **Opposite:** A detail showing the stems of Elizabethan holly braid stitch, worked in metallic passing, bordered with two lines of Elizabethan ladder braid worked in green silk.
> © *The Embroiderers' Guild*

ment of the coiling tendrils. Bright red berries dominate the design, and at some time in its past they inspired its association with holly berries, though Nevinson's original description of "a small currant twig" seems more appropriate. The main stems do not follow the usual circular path, but connect together in more of an a-shape. They are around 6 mm wide, and are formed from two lines of Elizabethan ladder braid stitch bordering a row of Elizabethan holly braid stitch. The Elizabethan ladder braid stitch has been worked in green silk, with around 14 stitches per centimetre (35 per inch). The Elizabethan holly braid stitch has been worked in metallic passing. The stitching is relatively open, varying between 2 to 3 mm in width, and averaging 5 stitches per centimetre (13 per inch).

More information:
Article in *Embroidery* Vol. 4 (1936)

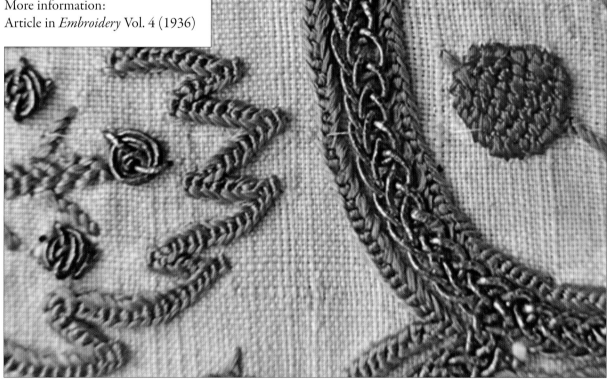

CASE STUDY 14

Example:
Elizabethan Plaited Braid Stitch- Standard (page 68)
Elizabethan Corded Detached Buttonhole (page 118)
Elizabethan Blanket Edging (page 100)
Object:
Coif
Location:
Heather Toomer Collection

Women's coifs of this style have been dated to the late 16th and early 17th century. The close fitting head covering is formed from a rectangle of fabric, cut so that two curves extend along each of the shorter sides. The embroidered fabric has been folded in half and stitched together along the top edge. When it was worn, the fold line would have sat at the back of the head, with the stitched seam on the top. The folded coif measures approximately 24 cm (9½ inch) in height, with a width of 17 cm (7½ inches), extending to 22 cm (8½ inch) at its widest. It is thought that the coif was adapted into a bag at some point in its life, as a straight lined crease and the remains of some stitching can be seen along the curved rim of the coif. It is possible that the three small tuft made from silk threads were inserted into the corners at this point.

The fabric was embroidered before the coif was constructed, in a design of repeating floral motifs encircled with coiling stems. A single moth or butterfly appears on each side. Although the design could be considered somewhat simplistic, it has been executed in tiny stitches on a fine close-set linen fabric, which has between 36 to 38 threads per linear centimetre (91-97 per inch). Thus, the lightweight fabric and dainty stitching gives the coif a refined delicacy.

The coiling stems are made from the standard version of Elizabethan plaited braid stitch worked in metallic passing. The gleam of the metallic thread is sharply contrasted by a border of little red silk stitches. These highlighting stitches are clustered together in sets of three, creating an impression of small thorns (page 90). The dimensions of the coiling stems are typical of surviving examples. The Elizabethan plaited braid stitch has a width of 3 mm, and 8 to 9 stitches along a centimetre length (20 -23 per inch). Small

Fig. 96. A close-up of the standard Elizabethan plaited braid stitch, edged with red silk stitching giving the impression of thorns. © *H. Toomer.*

86

Fig. 97. A lady's coif, decorated with coiling stems and simplistic floral motifs. There is evidence that the right-hand side was folded in and stitched together, possibly for re-use as a bag. © *H. Toomer.*

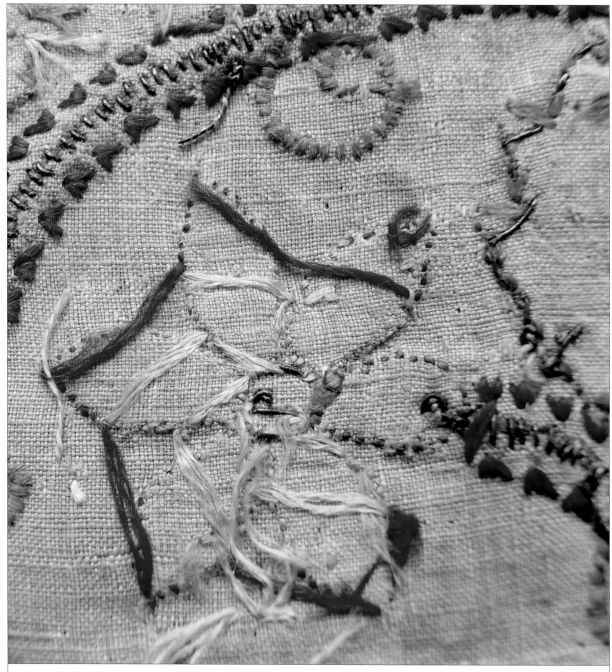

Fig. 98. A close-up detail showing the back of motifs made from Elizabethan detached buttonhole.
The front of the motifs can be seen on the opposite page. The stitching is taken into the fabric at the edge of the motif,
and forms the straight-forward turn described on page 119. Note the long floating stitches that take the coloured silk
from one petal tip to another, thus avoiding ending and starting a new thread. © *H. Toomer.*

tendrils periodically come out from the coiling stems. They are made from coral stitch (Fig. 113, page 104) worked in green silk with approximately 8-9 stitches along a centimetre length.

The flower and leaf motifs are Elizabethan corded detached buttonhole stitch worked in a fine thread made up of four strands of an S-twisted 2-ply silk. As only the edge of the thread catches into the fabric, little is wasted on the reverse of the embroidery. The stitching is dainty with around 12-13 stitches per centimetre length (30-33 per inch), and 12 rows of stitching per centimetre (30 per inch). Most of the motifs are made up from bands of contrasting colours, and a few include small stripes of metallic passing.

These straight-edged bands of colour are a usual outcome when using Elizabethan corded detached buttonhole stitch. The stitching is built up in linear rows, and because of the ease of changing colour at the start of a new row, there is a tendency to produce striped patterns on areas of this stitch type. The angular outline of the motifs is also a result of taking a straightforward route in shaping the lines of stitching. The gentle slopes are a consequence of not alternating the position of the loops at the edges, whilst the more exaggerated changes result from extended or reduced rows of stitching. One wonders whether the embroiderer actively selected these shapes that suit the stitch, or whether they adjusted motifs as the stitching progressed.

Fig. 99. The hemmed edges of the coif have been decorated with Elizabethan blanket stitches, worked in pink and green silk. The size of the stitches have been varied to produce an attractive pattern. © *H. Toomer.*

The raw edges of the linen fabric have all been folded into a seam, held in place with tiny stitches worked in linen thread. Decorative stitching has been worked over the top of all the seams, including the two that join at the top of the coif. A simple but effective border is constructed from Elizabethan blanket stitches worked in either a green or pink flossy silk thread. Each colour is worked alternately to create a cluster of three stitches, whilst the other non-active thread lies dormant beneath the stitching. Varying the width and depth of the stitches creates the little triangular pattern. Each cluster is formed from one deep stitch bordered by two shorter ones, and extends no more than 2 millimetres from the edge of the fabric. These three stitches are spaced close together, whilst a longer distance is left between each cluster, so that each repeat is approximately 4-5 millimetres in length.

"Thorn" stitches

The coiling stems are bordered with clusters of small stitches that resemble thorns. They are worked in red silk and follow the path illustrated below.

Bring the needle out of the fabric at position A. Take the needle downwards to the right, over the surface of the fabric, and enter the fabric at position B. Take the needle underneath the fabric to exit at position C, directly above position B. Bring the needle downwards and enter the fabric at D (on top of B). Take the needle underneath the fabric, up to the right and exit the fabric at position E. Bring the needle downwards to the left, over the surface of the fabric and enter the fabric at F (on top of D). Take the needle to the right, underneath the fabric, and exit the fabric to start another cluster of stitches.

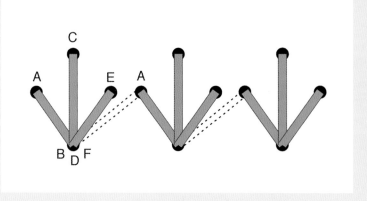

Fig. 100. A foxglove motif made from silk Elizabethan detached buttonhole stitch, and chain stitches worked in metallic passing. The surrounding stems, in standard Elizabethan plaited braid stitch, are edged with the red silk stitching. They resemble thorns and their path is illustrated on the opposite page. © *H. Toomer.*

CASE STUDY 15

Example:
Elizabethan Plaited Braid Stitch- Variation One (page 70)
Object:
Jacket
Location:
Victoria & Albert Museum, London
Accession Number:
T.228-1994

Various jackets of this type have survived, but the significance of this particular one is its provenance. The jacket belonged to Margaret Layton who died in 1641. The exact year of her birth is uncertain. It is thought that the jacket was made for Margaret around 1610, and she is seen wearing it in a portrait. The painting, which is also in the Victoria & Albert Museum collection (E.214-1994), has been attributed to Marcus Gheeraerts the Younger, and dated to around 1620.

The impact made by the jacket, both in the painting and in the flesh, is powerful. Costume played a significant role in exhibiting status, and there is no doubting that the jacket is an impressive piece. The linen fabric has been carefully tailored and lined with silk to produce a close-fitting garment. An embroidered design, of floral motifs encircled with coiling stems, has been worked over the entire surface. Each shaped linen section would have been embroidered separately before assembly. Although the design does not coordinate at the seams, the embroidery is arranged symmetrically about the front opening, though there are subtle differences between the two sides. The result is a profusion of coloured silk, metallic passing and scattered spangles. It is visually striking, but the jacket also represented a costly investment in materials and craftsmanship.

The importance of costume is reflected in the paintings of this era, as they depict garments in great detail. These images provide a rich source of information that supplements the lack of extant items. Having both Margaret's portrait and her actual garment, allows us a unique view of how accurately these textiles were represented. In addition, they illustrate how each can offer a different perspective. Access to the painting allows us to understand how the jacket was worn and combined with other garments. Whilst the actual jacket reveals intimate detail of how it was constructed and altered.

Unfortunately, with regards to embroidery, paintings provide limited information. Although the designs, colours and textures are graphically illustrated, it is not surprising that the finer elements, such as stitch detail, remain obscured. Margaret's portrait clearly represents the coiling stems worked in a gilt thread, but only close examination of the actual object reveals their true nature. Most of the coiling stems are made from Elizabethan plaited braid stitch (variation one). This stitch has also been used to cover the seams of the jacket. The subtle irregularity seen in the size and tension of the stitching has not diminished the impressive impact made by the jacket. Even the sections of coiling stem that have been worked in a different stitch are barely discernable.

More information:
Details and images about this jacket are available online in the Victoria & Albert "Search the Collection" database.

Fig. 101. Opposite: A detail of Margaret Layton's jacket showing Elizabethan plaited braid stitch (variation one) forming coiling stems and a covering over the straight seams.
© *Victoria & Albert Museum, London.*

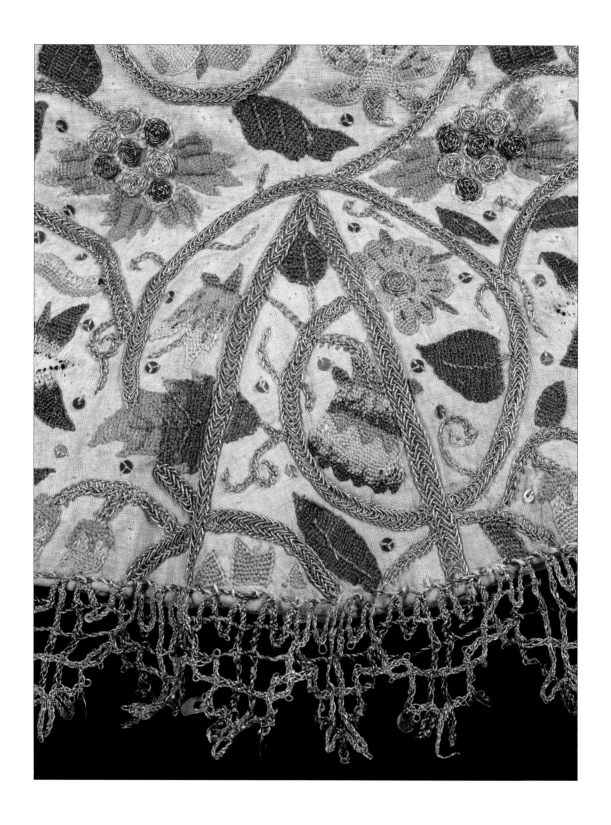

CASE STUDY 16

Example:
Elizabethan Plaited Braid Stitch - Variation Two (page 72)
Elizabethan Looped Edging (page 102)
Elizabethan Double Twisted Chain (page 108)
Elizabethan Corded Detached Buttonhole (page 118)
Object:
Book Cover
Location:
British Library, London
Shelfmark:
Davis 31

*T*he *Second Part of the Booke of Christian Exercise* by Robert Parsons contains religious instruction "guiding all men to their salvation". It is a petit book that sits comfortably in the palm of your hand, as it measures around 7½ by 13½ cm (3 x 5 inches), with a spine width of 3 cm (1 inch).

This particular copy has been encased in an embroidered cover, which has been personalised for its owners. On the front cover sits the arms of Henry, the first Baron Norris (or Norreys). The back cover depicts the arms of his wife, Margery (Margaret). Both knew Queen Elizabeth I when she was still a princess, and continued their friendship after her coronation, spending time at court and entertaining her at their home in Rycote.

The book was published in 1598, shortly before the death of Margery in 1599, and Henry in 1601. The embroidered design on the cover also features flowers, hazel nuts and another individual motif above each set of arms. On the front sits a black bird, and above the arms on the back is an angular motif reminiscent of a horizontal obelisk. The motifs have been worked in silk tent stitches, whilst small details have been highlighted in a range of different stitches, working in metallic passing. For instance, the fine lines seen on Henry's arms are an example of Elizabethan double twisted chain stitch. The lines are between 1 to 2 mm wide with 11-12 stitches per centimetre (28-30 per inch).

The motifs sit on an unusual background of Elizabethan corded detached buttonhole stitch, which is normally found filling the inside of a motif. Instead, here it has been moulded to fit around the outside contours of the motifs. The stitching has been worked from a single element of gilt passing, which enters the linen fabric at the end of each row. The stitching is relatively open, affording us a good view of the structure. Interestingly, the first row of stitching on the front cover is at the bottom of the book, whilst on the back cover it is at the top of the book. The two sections on Henry's arms flow in the opposite direction to the background, as they both start at the top of the shield. Along the first line of stitching, the loop of every stitch is taken into the fabric, passing neatly under (0:1) linen threads as if it were a needlepoint stitch. However, the linen fabric has around 13-14 stitches per linear centimetre (33-35 per inch) and there are roughly 10 stitches per centimetre (25 per inch) for the embroidery. Consequently, not all the linen gaps are filled along the straight-edged start, providing some of the inconsistencies that one starts to expect in historic pieces.

The first row of Elizabethan corded detached buttonhole stitch can seem a little sparse, so here an Elizabethan looped edging helps to add some volume. It was added afterwards using a metallic passing that matches the main stitching. This addition also creates a rounded edge that mimics the bottom row, and hides the short dashes created when the original stitching pierces the fabric. The Elizabethan looped edging does not pierce the fabric but works into the top row of the Elizabethan corded detached buttonhole stitch, passing over one or two threads (see Fig. 102).

The outer rim of the whole book is trimmed

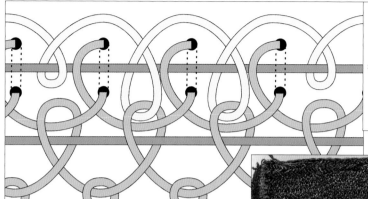

Fig. 102. Diagram of the Elizabethan looped edging worked into the top edge of the Elizabethan corded detached buttonhole stitch. The two stitches have been illustrated in different tones to highlight their structure. Note that the looped edging does not always sit uniformly through the lower stitching.

with a woven band made from metallic passing. A secondary border of embroidery surrounds the design on the front and back cover. This rectangular frame is made of Elizabethan plaited braid stitch (variation two), worked in metallic passing. The stitches are of average width at 3 mm wide, but are compact, with 13-14 stitches per centimetre (33-35 per inch). These straight lines of Elizabethan plaited braid stitch are worked as needlepoint with each stitch entering and exiting the fabric in a uniform manner between the linen threads. The stitch has also been used to decorate the spine, though here the stitch has been worked in two different metallic passing threads, and forms sinuous curves winding around a staff. The stitching is looser, ranging from 3 to 5 mm wide, with around 10 stitches per centimetre (25 per inch).

More information:
Images of the book cover are available online in the British Library's database of bookbindings.

Fig. 103. The front cover depicting the arms of Henry Norris.
© *British Library Board (Davis 31).*

CASE STUDY 17

Example:
Elizabethan Plaited Braid Stitch- Cherry (page 74)
Elizabethan Ladder (page 110)
Object:
Manuscript Cover
Location:
Bodleian Library, Oxford
Shelfmark:
MS Cherry 36

This iconic manuscript is famous because of its eleven-year old author, who grew up to become Queen Elizabeth I. *The Miroir or Glasse of the Synneful Soul* is Princess Elizabeth's handwritten translation of a French poem written by Marguerite de Navarre, sister of King Francis I of France. She presented it to Katherine Parr as a New Year's gift in 1544/5, and in the dedication Elizabeth apologises for any mistakes and asks her stepmother to correct them. The handwritten book is further personalised with an embroidered cover, also thought to be the work of Princess Elizabeth. As such, the gift would have made an ideal showcase for Elizabeth's talents and virtuous activity. The following year, Elizabeth presented two translations, with matching covers, to Katherine Parr and Henry VIII. There are similarities between all three embroidered covers, in both design and execution. However, the style of needlework is not typical when compared to other work dating from this period. Early 16th century book covers are more often decorated in applied ornamentation, whilst the needlepoint style appears to have been more popular in the early 17th century. The materials found on MS Cherry 36 are also atypical. The blue silk is highly twisted, with at least four plies S-twisted together. In addition, whilst the metallic threads resemble passing, the coils of flat strip, or round wire, do not sit neatly around their inner thread, but bulge away from their core.

The embroidered cover is worked as one piece, and edged with a narrow woven band around the entire rim. A stitched border, worked in red silk and metallic thread, divides the cover into three sections, separating the spine design from the front and back. The front measures approximately 18 x 13 cm (7 x 5 inch), with a spine depth of about 3 cm (1 inch). Both sides of the cover feature the same design with only minor changes in the stitching. Katherine Parr's initials sit at the centre of the design, surrounded by knotwork with a padded pansy in each corner. The stitches are well executed in spite of the unusual threads. The knotwork comprises two parts, each worked in a different stitch. An outline of connecting squares is made from Elizabethan ladder stitch. It has been worked with a core thread that sits loosely inside a tight coil of round gilt wire. The stitching is approximately 4 mm wide with 8 stitches per cm (20 per inch). The 'rungs' of the Elizabethan ladder stitch have been filled with a marginally finer thread that has the appearance of tarnished silver. These filling stitches are S-slanting back stitches that travel over two rungs before doubling back under one rung (see page 130). Within each square of the design sits a continuous four-looped motif that is reminiscent of Celtic knotwork as it interlaces through itself and the square. It is made from Elizabethan plaited braid stitch (Cherry version), using a core thread that sits loosely inside a tight coil of flattened metal. This stitching is approximately 3 mm wide with 8-9 stitches per cm (20-23 per inch).

More information:
Details are available on-line at the Bodelian Library.

Fig. 104. Opposite. The front cover of the manuscript MS. Cherry 36, made by Queen Elizabeth I when she was eleven. © *The Bodleian Library, University of Oxford.*

Fig. 105. A close-up of the coif in Case Study 22 (page 144). Coiling stems of Elizabethan plaited braid stitch (variation one) encircle a pansy motif of Elizabethan corded detached buttonhole stitch, with bordered turns.
The change in colour provides evidence that the raised edge and the internal stitches are worked simultaneously.
© Witney Antiques

Looped stitches

This section looks at a collection of stitches that are not normally gathered together in the same grouping. Nonetheless, they are related as they are all constructed from loops of thread that are made using the same basic action (see below). The loops can be connected together in different ways and it is this that produces the variation. As mentioned on page 6, the examination of historic embroidery revealed a persistent recurrence of loops with Z-slanting crossovers. This suggests that the original stitches were worked from bottom-to-top, left-to-right.

Looped stitches can be formed with the loops working into the fabric, or they can be made over the surface, with the thread only passing through the fabric at the end of each sequence. Alternatively, they can be worked *punto in aria* (stitches in air), and attached onto the fabric when complete (see page 122 for more details of term). However, the boundary between these three types appeared to be very fluid in historical examples. Accordingly, it has been decided to arrange the stitches in an alternative way, depending how the loops connect to one another. In order to help identify certain aspects of the stitches, a loop will be referred to as having *arms*. These are the straight sections just before and after the circular form of the loop. If the arms of two loops connect together then a *rung* is formed between them.

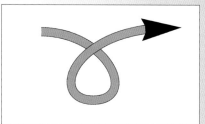

Fig. 106. The same loop action creates all the stitches in this section. The two straight sections to the top left and right will be referred to as *arms*. They crossover in a Z-slant as they become the loop.

The loops of the first few stitches (page 100-105) are only connected together by their arms and they need to be supported by the fabric or other stitching. The next group of stitches (page 106-117) join themselves together by taking the new loop behind a loop from the previous row. There follows a selection of stitches (page 118-125) that are all connected by taking new loops over the rungs of the previous stitches, and finally the last group (page 126-129) have new loops taken through the loops of the previous row.

Generally, for all the stitches in this section it is best not to apply an excessive amount of tension, especially at the start of the stitching. This is because the needle will need sufficient room to pass beneath or through your previous stitching. Working with metallic passing thread will automatically help to keep the stitch structure firm but open. However, when using silk remember not to pull too tight. As with most stitches, there is an optimum arrangement of the stitches that will vary depending on the thread you are working with, so be prepared to test your tensioning to get the best results.

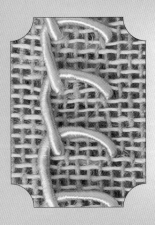

Elizabethan blanket stitch

Today, blanket stitch is the name given to widely spaced button-hole stitches, especially if worked over an edge (see Fig 109). The result is not the same as the Elizabethan version. No matter which way it is viewed - turned upside down, or seen from the reverse - the modern stitch structure does not match those seen on historic pieces. Therefore, the embroiderers of old used a different method. Working from bottom-to-top, left-to-right generates an accurate reproduction of the Z-slanting crossover, and though subjective, practical experiment determined that this method actually felt more comfortable than modern practice. With the edge of the fabric uppermost, gravity held the bulk of the fabric in one's lap, and afforded a clear view down onto the work in progress.

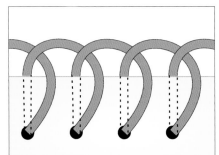

Fig 107. Structure of Elizabethan blanket stitch.

The historic stitch was found used as both a functional and decorative edging stitch, so the initial set of instructions has been written with the assumption that the embroidery was held in the hand. However, Elizabethan blanket stitches were also found worked onto the fabric's surface, forming stems or decorative edges around motifs, so there follows some addition instruction for working on a frame.

An example of Elizabetathan blanket stitch is illustrated in Case Study 14 (page 86), Case Study 18 (page 133) and Case Study 22 (page 144).

Fig. 108. Detail from Case Study 18 (page 133), showing coiling stems surrounding rose motifs. The stems are bordered with Elizabethan blanket stitch giving the appearance of thorns.
© Witney Antiques

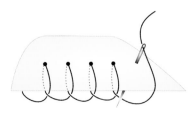

Fig. 109. Modern blanket stitch.

A Start

Hold the fabric in your left hand with the edge uppermost. Ideally, secure the beginning of the thread within the seam so that it is hidden for view. Start with the thread on the left-hand side, coming up from behind the edge.

Stitching over an edge

Step One:
Bring the needle over the top edge and to the front of the fabric, so that the thread forms an arch, from left-to-right and over the edge of the fabric.

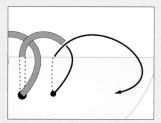

Step Two:
Take the needle into the fabric to the right of the previous entry hole. As the needle emerges from the back of the fabric, make sure that it passes over the arch of thread made in step one.

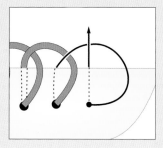

A finish

Secure the thread after step two, close to the top of the stitch and preferably hidden within the edge seam.

Stitching on a frame

Step One:
Surface section - Bring the needle to the right, so that the thread forms an arch going from top-left to bottom-right. Enter the fabric to the right of the previous entry point.

Step Two:
Underneath section - Take the needle underneath the fabric in a straight line from bottom-to-top, and exit the fabric to the right of the previous exit point. Make sure that the needle exits to the left of the arch of thread made in step one.

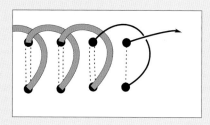

Shaping

The size of the stitch can be adjusted by altering the position of the entry holes. Increasing or decreasing the space between each hole (X) will widen or narrow the stitch, whilst varying the distance between the hole and the edge of the fabric (Y) will change the depth of the stitch.

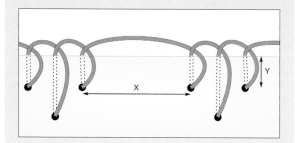

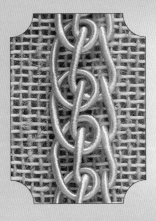

Elizabethan looped edging

As with the previous stitch, the Elizabethan looped edging also forms a row of loops that are only connected together by their arms. Unlike Elizabethan blanket stitch, this version does not enter the background fabric. The thread remains on the surface by working through existing stitching, thus forming a composite stitch. Elizabethan looped edging was found added to various different stitches, with each combination producing a distinctive affect. It was a popular and useful edging that could be attached afterwards to improve the appearance of other stitches. For instance, it was used to highlight and smooth the edges of Elizabethan corded Brussels (Fig. 92, page 81), and to make a more uniform start to Elizabethan corded detached buttonhole (Fig. 102, page 95).

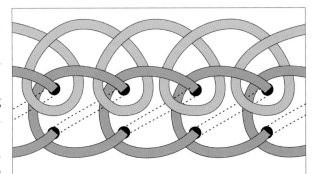

Fig. 110. Structure of Elizabethan looped edging worked onto chain stitch.

In each instance the method remains basically the same, except for the exact route the looping takes through the initial stitching. One of the most common combinations found on surviving items is the one illustrated here. It consists of a preliminary line of chain stitches. The edging is then added afterwards, onto one side of the chain stitching. Many, but not all, historic examples were found with the thread turning at the end of the chain stitching, so that the edging started directly afterward using the same thread. When worked in metallic passing, the thread naturally curves to hold open the loops. The edging is taken around every overlap of two chain stitches. This tends to lift the sides of the chain stitches, creating a raised ridge at the centre of the composite stitching. If the two parts of the composite stitch are worked evenly, it can be difficult to distinguish the chain stitch from the edging.

An example of Elizabetathan looped edging is illustrated in Case Study 12 (page 76) and Case Study 16 (page 94).

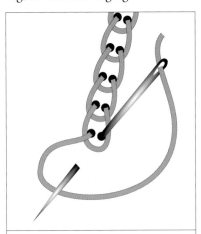

Fig. 111. Modern chain stitch.

A Start

You will need an initial line of chain stitches (see Fig. 111). Remember to leave sufficient space between each stitch, so that there is room to add the edging. To start the edging, either secure a new thread at the end of the line, or simply continue with the same thread you used for the chain stitching.

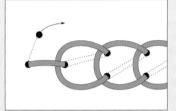

Stitching from left-to-right

Step One:
Surface section - Bring the needle to the right, so that the thread forms an arch above the stitching. Take the needle downward into the next empty chain stitch, going under just the topmost section of this stitch.

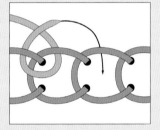

Step Two:
Surface section - Bring the needle to the left, so that it goes over a section of the chain stitch, and between the exit/entry points of the previous chain stitch. Take the needle upwards, going under the topmost section of the previous chain stitch. Make sure it stays to the right of the previous edging stitch. Keep the needle above the arch of thread created in step one.

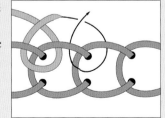

A finish

Take the needle into the fabric, close to the chain stitching. Secure the thread underneath in a concealed position.

Shaping

Any shaping applied to the underlying chain stitch will automatically shape the edging as it follows the contours of the initial stitching.

Elizabethan double looped edging

This is a denser version of the looped edging as the loops are arranged so that they overlap one another. As with the previous stitch, the looped thread does not pierce the fabric, but is worked around other stitching. Once again, the edging can be applied onto different stitches to produce various effects. Here, a line of coral stitches has been selected to produce the initial stitching. Coral stitch is illustrated below, but these stitches have been simplified in the other diagrams so that the focus is on the edging. The loops of the edging create an S-crossing, the opposite to the usual format

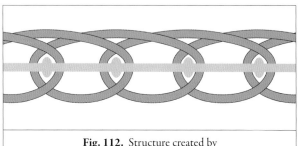

Fig. 112. Structure created by Elizabethan double looped edging.

seen in this section. However, the structure is easily recreated by using the action that consistently takes the needle underneath all of the threads. This action lends itself to taking the thread through all of the initial stitching, so that the looped thread appears on both sides. The overlap of the loops can make the two sides appear a little imbalanced, with the upper edge producing a denser edging than the lower side. This tends to get exaggerated when Elizabethan double looped edging is added onto shaped stitching. If the denser side of the edging sits on the outer rim of a curve, then the imbalance appears to be intensified (see Fig. 114).

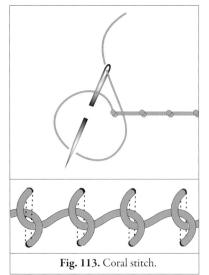

Fig. 113. Coral stitch.

An example of Elizabetathan double looped edging is illustrated in Case Study 19 (page 135).

A finish

Take the needle into the fabric, and secure the thread underneath in a concealed position.

Shaping

Any shaping applied to the underlying coral stitch will automatically shape the edging as it follows the contours of the initial stitching.

A Start

You will need an initial line of coral stitches (see Fig. 113). Remember to leave sufficient space between each stitch, so that there is room to add the edging. To start the edging, either secure a new thread at the end of the line, or simply continue with the same thread you used for the coral stitching.

Fig. 114. Close-up of Case Study 19 (page 135) showing the blue coral stitching and the gilt Elizabethan double looped edging. Note the distortion of the edging as it follows the curved coral stitching.
© *Privately owned. Copyright in the image reserved to the owner.*

Stitching from left-to-right

Step One:
Surface section - Bring the needle to the right, along to the next empty space between the exit/entry points of the coral stitching. Take the needle downward going underneath the single thread.

Step Two:
Surface section - Bring the needle to the left, so that it passes the exit/entry points of two coral stitches. Take the needle upwards, going underneath a total of four threads: the bottom of the previous loop, a thread from the coral stitching, and two threads of the previous loop.
Continue repeating the two steps.

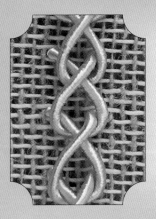

Elizabethan twisted chain stitch

The following looped stitches (page 106-117) constitute a subgroup because they are all constructed by passing the needle behind the loops of previous stitches. In order to enable identification they will be referred to as *Ceylon-style* stitches. Elizabethan twisted chain can be considered the first of this group as it forms a single column of loops, with the needle passing behind just one loop of the previous stitching.

Elizabethan twisted chain differs from the modern version (Fig. 116) in both its structure and in its presumed manner of making. The modern stitch produces a cross at the base of the loop, but the upper section is angled at an S-slant, rather than in the Z-slant seen on historic versions. Also, only one end of the modern stitch sits within the previous loop, whereas the Elizabethan stitch has both ends enclosed in a loop that is actually the subsequent stitch. The method shown here is worked in a manner that relates to modern *reverse*, or *broad*, chain (Fig. 117), in that a new loop is created by taking the needle back through previous stitching, rather than making the new loop around the needle. This manner of working applies to

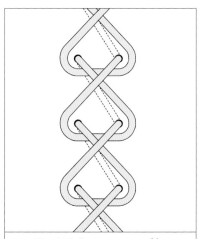

Fig. 115. Structure created by Elizabethan twisted chain stitch.

all the Ceylon-style stitches. Examples were usually found worked in metallic passing, as the firm thread helps to hold open the looped structure. In spite of this, it is worth remembering that the needle will need to pass back underneath your surface sections stitching, so do not tension too firmly, especially when making a start.

When making Elizabethan twisted chain one can vary the size of the stitching by altering where the needle exits and enters the fabric. The distance between pairs of exit/entry points will elongate the stitches, whilst increasing the space between the exit and entrance points will widen the stitch. There comes a point at which this broadening starts to distort the structure, and long arms are formed when the exit and entry points no longer sit within the subsequent stitch. This extended version of Elizabethan twisted chain resembles modern Vandyke stitch (Fig. 118), except that the historic version is worked bottom-to-top to produce a Z-slant crossover. The same affect can be applied to all of the following Ceylon-style stitches.

An example of Elizabetathan twisted chain stitch is illustrated in Case Study 20 (page 139).

Fig. 116. Modern twisted chain.

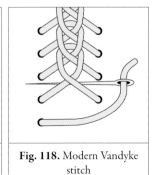

Fig. 117. Modern reverse chain.

Fig. 118. Modern Vandyke stitch

106

A start

Bring the needle out of the fabric at A. Take it over the surface, down to the right, and enter the fabric at B. Take the needle underneath the fabric, from right-to-left, and exit at C. Bring the needle up to the right over the thread section AB and enter the fabric at D. Take the needle underneath the fabric, up to the left and exit at E, ready to start working normally.

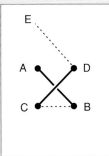

A finish

Finish after step two and secure the thread underneath the fabric in a concealed position.

Shaping

Straight lines are achieved by working the exit and entry points in straight parallel lines. To curve the stitching to the left, exit the fabric (in this instance, in step three) slightly lower and further to the left than usual. In addition, enter the fabric (in this instance, in step two) slightly higher and further to the left than usual. The entry/exit holes are arranged like the ones seen in Fig. 71 (page 63). To curve the stitching to the right, make the same adjustments, but to the right rather left.

Stitching from bottom-to-top

Step One:
Surface section - Bring the needle down towards you and to the right of the stitching. Take the needle from right-to-left under the previous loop, so that it passes under two threads just below the exit/entry points.

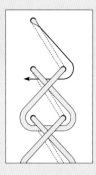

Step Two:
Surface section - Bring the needle up to the right, so that it crosses over itself to form a new loop. Take the needle into the fabric a little above the previous entry point.

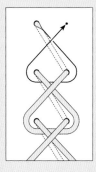

Step Three:
Underneath section - Bring the needle underneath the fabric, up to the left, and exit at a point just above the previous exit point.
Continue repeating the three steps.

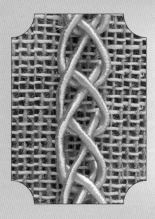

Elizabethan double twisted chain stitch

Elizabethan double twisted chain is a denser version of a one-column looped stitch, and is created by taking the needle back behind two of the previous stitches, rather than one. When working back behind two stitches, subtle differences in the angle of the stitching can affect the number of threads that each stitch crosses over and under. As mentioned on page 106, the position of the exit and entrance holes can also change the appearance of this stitch, as they can sit wider apart so that the arms start to extend out beyond the loops. The version illustrated here was found to be the most common one seen on examined items. Notice that the end of each loop has been lengthened, so that one arm is longer than the other. A minimal amount of thread is used underneath the fabric because the end of one loop and the start of another sit close together, both within the loop of the subsequent stitch. This contrasts with Elizabethan twisted chain, where the start and end of the same loop sit within the loop of the subsequent stitch.

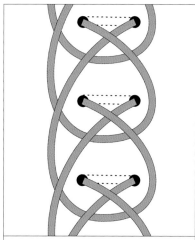

Fig. 119. Structure created by Elizabethan double twisted chain stitch.

The Ceylon-style stitches were usually found worked flat onto the fabric's surface, but they were also seen stitched over seamed edges to form a neat decorative and protective border. Under these circumstances the exit and entry points of the stitching could be considered as the same hole, one either side of the edge. The instructions for making an edging, rather than flat stitch, are the same except the surface sections are worked over the lip of the fabric's edge. In addition, the last step that brings the needle from right to left underneath the fabric becomes redundant. The needle enters to the right of the stitching on one side of the fabric, and emerges to the left of the stitching on the other side of the fabric, thus making it a single action.

An example of Elizabetathan double twisted chain stitch is illustrated in Case Study 16 (page 94).

Fig. 120. Elizabethan double twisted chain can be worked over the edge of fabric. In these circumstances the needle enters and exits the fabric in one movement, passing from one side of the fabric to the other as shown above. The same principle can be applied to other Ceylon-style stitches, and an example can be seen in Fig. 52 (page 49).

A start

Bring the needle out of the fabric at A, and make a short surface section going bottom-to-top and enter the fabric at B. Take the needle underneath the fabric and exit at C. Bring the needle down to the right, over the surface. Enter the fabric at D, to the right of AB. Take the needle underneath the fabric from right-to-left and exit the fabric at E, to the left of AB. Bring the needle over the surface, up to the right. Enter the fabric at F, above and to the right of C. Take the needle underneath the fabric from right-to-left and exit at G ready to start working normally. In step one, the first stitch will pass above ADE, but below B.

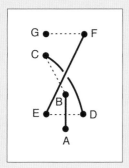

A finish

Complete step two and secure the thread beneath the fabric.

Shaping

As with Elizabethan twisted chain, page 107.

Stitching from bottom-to-top

Step One:
Surface section - Bring the needle down towards you and to the right of the stitching. Take the needle to the point just below the two most recent entry points. Pass the needle under the stitching, going from right-to-left, perpendicular to the stitching, so that it passes under three threads and arrives on the left-hand side just below two exit points (one is the start point of this stitch).

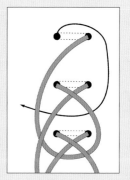

Step Two:
Surface section - Bring the needle up to the right, so that it crosses over itself to form a new loop. Take the needle into the fabric a little above the previous entry point.

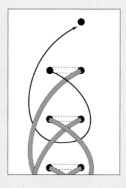

Step Three:
Underneath section - Bring the needle from right-to-left underneath the fabric, and exit the fabric a little above the previous exit point. Continue repeating the three steps.

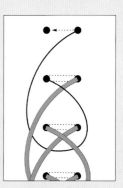

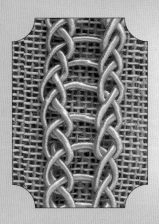

Elizabethan ladder stitch

Here repeated actions create two columns of loops. The stitch sequence forms a pair of loops, each with one short and one long arm. The two longer arms join together to form *rungs* that connect the two columns of the ladder stitch. Generally, the shorter arms sit within the subsequent stitch, as seen in Elizabethan twisted chain, though some examples had arms that extended outwards like a Vandyke stitch (Fig. 118. page 106).

Once again the modern version differs from the original examples as the threads cross themselves in the opposite direction. In addition, the historic versions were usually more than just a ladder framework, as extra stitching was frequently seen augmenting the rungs in the central gap between the loops. Many variations of the ladder stitch have been found, caused by differences in the underlying structure and the choice of central filling. Three terms have been assigned to differentiate the connections used to make the Ceylon-style stitches. *Single* refers to loops taken behind just one loop of the previous stitching, as seen in Elizabethan twisted chain. *Double* refers to a loop taken behind two previous stitches in the same manner as illustrated in Elizabethan double twisted chain stitch. The path shown for double appears to be the most common route, so other loops that are also taken behind two previous stitches but in a slightly different path will be referred to as *variations*. The historic examples of ladder stitches were not always formed of matching columns, for instance the first column might be single whilst the second is double. The simplest combination is illustrated here, and consists of a 'single/single' ladder, where the loops in both columns work around just one previous stitch, and there are no central additions. Additional filling stitches will be illustrated separately as they can be applied to any ladder type, as well as other Ceylon-style stitches (see page 130).

An example of Elizabetathan ladder stitch is illustrated in Case Study 17 (page 96).

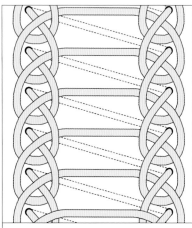

Fig. 121. The structure created by Elizabethan ladder stitch.

Fig. 122. Left: The two stages of making a *single* loop. The new loop works 'over one, under two', before turning and going 'over two' threads.
Centre: The two stages of making a *double* loop. The new loop works 'over two, under three', before turning and going 'over two' threads.
Right: The two stages of making a *variation* loop. The new loop works "over two, under four' before turning and 'over three' threads.

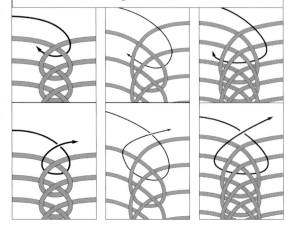

A Start

Bring the needle out of the fabric at A. Make a surface section going top-to-bottom and enter the fabric at B. Take the needle underneath the fabric to the left of A, and exit at C.

Bring the needle down, over the surface, and enter the fabric at D. Take the needle underneath the fabric up to the left, and exit at E, ready to start working normally. The first Elizabethan ladder stitch (EF) is taken behind the two surface sections AB and CD, instead of behind the loops of the previous stitch.

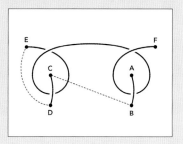

A finish

At step three, enter the fabric in a more central position, just above the last rung and secure the thread at the back of the fabric.

Shaping

As with Elizabethan twisted chain, page 107.

Stitching from bottom-to-top

Step One:
Surface section - Bring the needle down to the right of the first column of loops. Take the needle from right-to-left, going under the previous loop (the thread passes over one rung before going under two threads).

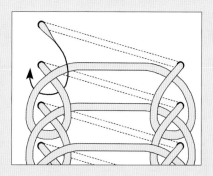

Step Two:
Surface section - Bring the needle up and to the right so that it crosses over itself to form a new loop. Take the needle to the right of the right-hand column of loops, and take the needle from right-to-left, going under the previous loop (passing under two threads).

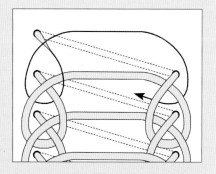

Step Three:
Surface section - Bring the needle up and to the right so that it crosses over two rungs and forms a new loop in the right-hand column. Enter the fabric directly above the previous entry point.

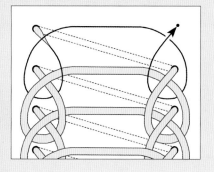

Step Four:
Underneath section - Bring the needle from right-to-left underneath the fabric, and exit the fabric directly above the previous exit point.

Continue repeating the four steps.

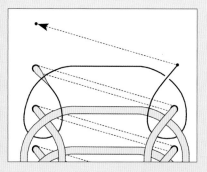

Elizabethan double ladder stitch

L
ike the previous stitch, this version also has matching columns, though here they are both worked as *double,* so the result is denser. The structure can look quite different depending on the position of the entry/exit points, as the arms can extend outwards adding to the complexity of the overlapping threads.

As mentioned on page 110 the term double has been selected to illustrate the version that was most commonly found on examined items. However it should be noted that when using this method, the new loop does not pass fully behind both previous loops. As the new loop comes down over the right-hand side of the column, it crosses over the right-hand arms of both previous loops, but as it goes behind them it stops short of going behind the left-hand arm of the second loop, so that when it arches up to the right it only goes over the arm of one previous loop (see Fig. 122 bottom centre). Examples where found that went fully behind two loops as shown in Fig. 122 (bottom right), but these were not found as frequently, possibly because they can seem a little asymmetric. If one follows the path made by each new loop, it can be seen that the double version is the most balanced of the three examples shown in Fig. 122. These diagrams apply to all the Ceylon-style group of stitches, though one has to remember that at the edges the size of the arms may be shortened, so that one barely notices that the new loop goes over them.

An example of Elizabetathan double ladder stitch is illustrated in Case Study 21 (page 140).

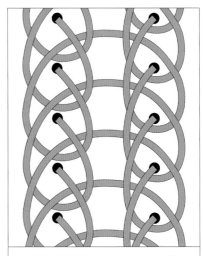

Fig. 123. The structure created by Elizabethan double ladder stitch.

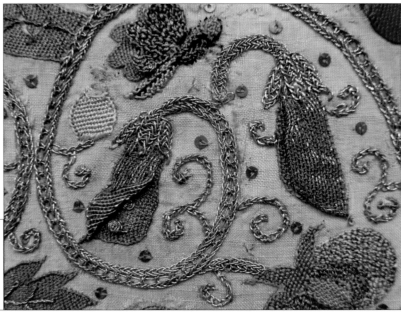

Fig. 124. Detail of a peapod motif from Case Study 21 (page 140). The coiling stem is Elizabethan double ladder stitch with a filling stitch.
© *Embroiderers' Guild*

A start

Bring the needle out of the fabric at A. Make a loose surface section arching upwards and enter the fabric at B. Take the needle underneath the fabric, and exit at C, midway between AB. Bring the needle up over the surface, and go over AB before entering the fabric at D. Take the needle underneath the fabric to the right, and exit at E. Bring the needle down to the left, going over the stitch section AB. Continue to the left, going underneath CD and AB. Arch the thread clockwise, up over D and to the right of E.

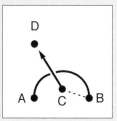

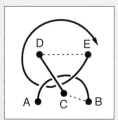

Make a clockwise loop around E, by taking the needle underneath two threads (the stitch section AB, and the thread coming down from E), and over two threads (the stitch section AB, and the thread arching over DE). Enter the fabric at F, and take the needle underneath the fabric to the left, and exit at G ready to start working normally.
The first stitch will pass behind the start stitching as shown.

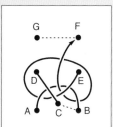

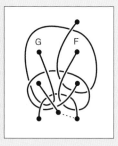

A finish

At step three enter the fabric in a more central position, just above the last rung and secure the thread at the back of the fabric.

Shaping

As with Elizabethan twisted chain (page 107).

Stitching from bottom-to-top

Step One:
Surface section - Bring the needle down to the right of the first column of loops, passing over two rungs of the previous stitching. Take the needle from right-to-left, going under three threads. Note that the needle passes below two exit points (one is part of the new loop).

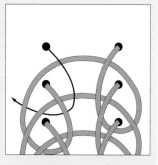

Step Two:
Surface section - Bring the needle up and to the right so that it forms a new loop.

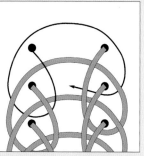

Bring the needle to the right of the right-hand column of loops, and take the needle from right-to-left, going under three threads. Note that the needle passes below two entry points.

Step Three:
Surface section - Bring the needle up and to the right so that it crosses over two rungs and forms a new loop in the right-hand column. Enter the fabric directly above the previous entry point.

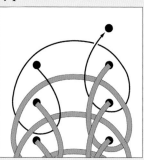

Step Four:
Underneath section - Bring the needle from right-to-left underneath the fabric, and exit the fabric directly above the previous exit point.

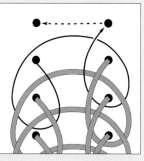

Continue repeating the four steps

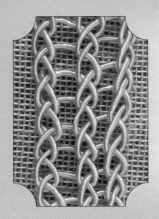

Elizabethan Ceylon stitch

The sub-group of Ceylon-style stitches, with their columns of Z-crossing loops, can be expanded further, by adding more loops in each row so that the number of columns is increased. Modern Ceylon stitch is recorded in various sizes, but all have S-slanting crossovers, and connect behind a single loop. The historic examples were typically made from three or four columns of loops, and as with the other Ceylon-style stitches these columns could be constructed from any combination of single, double or variation connections. Here, the instructions are given for a three-column version of the stitch, with each column making a single connection. Surviving examples were usually made from metallic passing, and were generally found forming coiling stems or seam coverings.

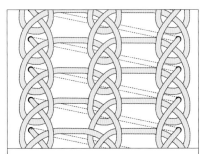

Fig. 125. The structure created by Elizabethan Ceylon stitch

An example of Elizabetathan Ceylon stitch is illustrated in Case Study 3 (page 49).

A start

Bring the needle out of the fabric at A. Take the needle over the surface to the right and enter the fabric at B. Take the needle underneath the fabric, from right-to-left and exit at C. Make a loose stitch section over the surface by taking the needle to the right, over AB, and enter the fabric at D. Take the needle underneath the fabric, from right-to-left and exit at E. Make a loose stitch section over the surface by taking the needle to the right, over CD, and enter the fabric at F. Take the needle underneath the fabric, from right-to-left and exit at G. Take the needle to the right, over EF, and enter the fabric at H. Take the needle underneath the fabric, from right-to-left and exit at I.

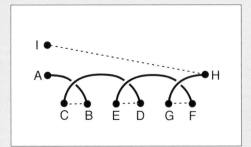

You are now ready to start working normally. Note that for step one the needle will pass behind the threads just above BC.

Stitching from bottom-to-top

Step One:
Bring the needle towards you, to the right of the first column of loops. Take the needle from right-to-left, going under the previous loop (the thread passes over one rung before going under two threads).

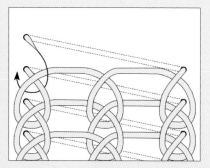

Step Two:
Bring the needle up and to the right of the second column of loops so that it crosses over itself to form a new loop. Take the needle from right-to-left, going under the previous loop of the middle column (the thread passes over one rung before going under two threads).

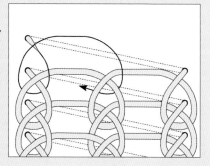

Step Three:
Bring the needle up and to the right of the third column (it will cross over two threads and form a new loop in the middle column). Take the needle from right-to-left, going under the previous loop of the right-hand column (the thread passes under two threads).

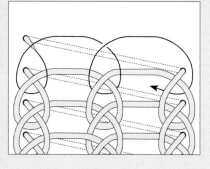

Step Four:
Bring the needle up and to the right (it will cross over two threads and form a new loop in the right-hand column. Enter the fabric directly above the previous entry point.

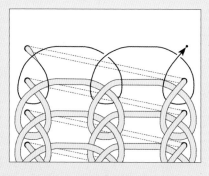

Step Five:
Bring the needle from right-to-left underneath the fabric, and exit directly above the previous exit point.

Continue repeating the five steps

A finish

Finish after step four, and take the needle underneath the fabric to exit the fabric at A, just above the right-hand rung. Take the needle down over the right-hand rung and into the fabric at B. Bring the needle underneath the fabric from right-to-left and exit the fabric at C, just above the last left-hand rung. Bring the needle down over the rung, and enter the fabric at D.

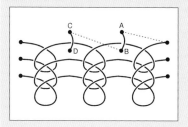

Shaping

As with Elizabethan twisted chain (page 107).

Elizabethan tubular Ceylon stitch

Although this stitch is three-dimensional and worked 'in the air' (see page 122), it is a direct continuation of the Ceylon-style stitches. The loops are connected together in the same manner as the previous stitches, but here they are worked in rows that spiral on top of one another. The resultant tubular structure was found on surviving textiles, forming insect bodies and raised floral sections, notably parts of honeysuckle flowers. The stitches were not worked onto the background fabric, but were made separately and attached afterwards with a different thread. Elizabethan tubular Ceylon stitch was also seen forming a covering over small tassel heads. It is possible to make this structure using a pronged tool, but the method shown here is more suitable for recreating the fine scale of the historic work. Typically, the examples comprised six to eight columns of stitching made from metallic passing, and measured less than 5mm in diameter.

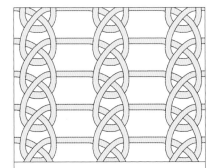

Fig. 126. Structure created by Elizabethan tubular Ceylon (just one surface of this tubular shape is shown).

An example of Elizabetathan tubular Ceylon stitch is illustrated in Case Study 4 (page 52) and Case Study 24 (page 149).

A start

Wind the thread around the thin rod. Make a few turns anti-clockwise, so that the thread goes from right-to-left behind the rod, and left-to-right in front.

Work the first loop of the first column by taking the needle from bottom-to-top under the turns around the rod, but over itself at the top.

Move to the right, turning the rod slightly, and start the first loop of the second column in exactly the same way. Continue round to the right making as many columns as required.

When you reach the first loop, you are ready to start the second loop of the first column, by working in the usual manner.

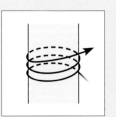 

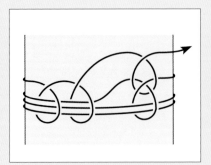

Stitching from bottom-to-top

Step One:
Take the needle to the right of the next column of loops. Bring the needle down and take it from right-to-left, going under the previous loop in this column (the thread passes over one rung before going under two threads).

Step Two:
Bring the needle up and to the right, so that it goes over two rungs to form a new loop in the column.

Continue repeating the two steps.

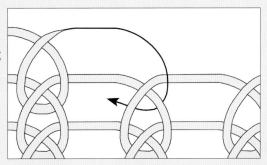

A finish

Remove the stitching from the rod. The tubular structure can be left open at the top, or you can make a couple of stitches across the opening to draw it together. Take the thread back through the stitching to secure it. Couch the tubular section in place onto the fabric using a separate fine thread.

Shaping

Typically this stitch was used to make short lengths of tubular stitching, and was not shaped. However, one can taper or increase the diameter of the stitching, either by omitting a column to reduce the size, or by adding a new loop onto a rung to start a new column for enlarging the dimensions.

Fig. 127. A close-up from Case Study 4 (page 52), showing a creature made from Elizabethan tubular Ceylon with a filling stitch worked over the rungs. Two black beads have been used for its eyes, and its legs have been created from additional black stitching worked into the fabric. © *The Embroiderers' Guild*

Elizabethan corded detached buttonhole stitch

Today, *detached buttonhole stitch* is well known. It consists of looped stitches connected over the rungs of the previous row (see Fig 129). The same structure is referred to as *single Brussels* in needlelace. Both are made top-to-bottom, with the rows worked left-to-right, then right-to-left, so that the lines of loops alternate between S- and Z-slanting crossovers. There is a difference between the embroidered and needlelace versions in that the former is made on the fabric, with the thread passing in and out of the background or border stitches at the end of every row, whereas the needlelace is made separately and does not pass through any fabric. Nevertheless, needlelace can be found on fabric, creating what is known as *raised* or *stumpwork*, but this is attached afterwards with a separate thread.

Fig 128. Structure created by Elizabethan corded detached buttonhole stitch

Elizabethan corded detached buttonhole stitch was a popular stitch, frequently seen filling motifs on historic items. These examples are usually described as detached buttonhole stitch. However, the historic stitch structure is not that seen in Fig 129. Many variations of buttonhole stitch can be found in modern embroidery books, but a corded version is more often documented as a needlelace stitch known as *corded Brussels stitch* (see page 122). Unlike modern versions, the Elizabethan stitch is composed of rows of loops, all with Z-slanting crossovers. The loops connect around the rungs of the previous row, and around a straight line of thread that runs from one edge to the other. This straight line not only adds body to the filling but also improves the ease of production. It takes the thread from one side to the other, allowing all the loops to be worked in the same direction. Here, the method is shown working bottom-to-top in keeping with the other historic stitches, so the Z-slanting crossovers naturally occur on the left-to-right row, and the straight line follows on the right-to-left row.

Although it was stated (page 7) that only one option would be shown for each stitch, here two different types of turn are illustrated because they can change the character of the motif. The first option is the most

Fig 129. Structure created by either modern detached buttonhole stitch or single Brussels stitch.

straightforward as the thread simply enters the fabric and exits a short distance above, ready to start the next row. The second option can create the visual impression of a frame around the edge, hence it is named a *bordered turn*. At first sight it appears as if the resultant motifs have been worked onto an outline created from chain or stem stitches, in much the same way as modern practice. However, here the 'border' is integral with the rest of the Elizabethan corded detached buttonhole, and can be observed in the way the edges change in multicoloured motifs (see Fig. 105, page 98). It is worth reading the shaping instructions when considering the turns, as these also play an important role in altering the appearance of the motif's edging, and can enhance the bordered turns. The use of gentle shaping was a common feature seen on historical motifs, with the stitching gradually increasing or decreasing as the rows turned at the edge.

An example is illustrated in Case Study 12 (page 76), 14 (page 86), 21 (page 122) and 22 (page 144).

A start

Secure the thread and bring it to the surface at the bottom-right of the motif, position A. Take the needle over the surface of the fabric from right-to-left and enter the fabric at the bottom-left of the motif, position B. Take the needle a short distance underneath the fabric and exit at position C, ready to start working a series of Elizabethan blanket stitches (see page 100) over the thread AB. You are then ready to start working normally by making a turn on the right-hand side.

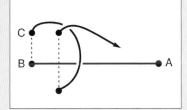

Stitching from left-to-right

Step One:
Surface section - bring the needle down to the right, going over two threads (the straight thread and a rung). Take the needle into the gap between the loops.

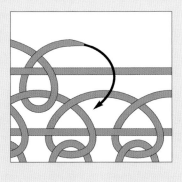

Step Two:
Surface section - bring the needle up and under two threads (the same ones as in step one). Then bring the needle out over the working thread so that a new loop is formed.

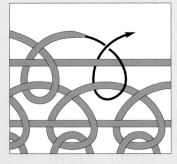

Turning on the right-hand side

As the row of loops reaches the right-hand side, take the needle into the fabric above the previous exit point. Bring the needle underneath the fabric from bottom-to-top, and exit the fabric a short distance from the entry point.

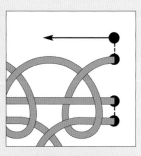

Stitching from right-to-left

Step One:
Surface section - Bring the needle to the left of the motif, so that the thread forms a straight line just above the previous stitching. Take the needle into the fabric just above the previous exit point.

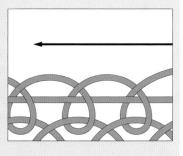

Turning on the left-hand side

Bring the needle underneath the fabric from bottom-to-top, and exit the fabric a short distance from the entry point.

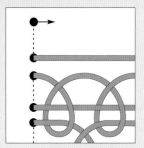

Shaping

A gentle form of shaping occurs as the thread turns at the end of the row. At each edge one has to decide which gap to use for the first and last looped stitch. The gaps marked 'X' are the closest to the edge, but are created by only one arm, whereas the gaps marked 'Y' are the first full-sized ones, formed from a pair of connecting arms that create a rung. Working into the half gaps marked X will gradually increase the stitching outwards, whilst working into the full gaps marked Y will decrease the stitching.

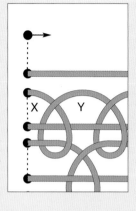

Parallel edges are achieved by stitching the same number of loops in each row. Straight edges that sit perpendicularly to the rows are made by alternately staggering the position of the first and last loop. Thus a row made with the first loop worked into X on the left-hand side, will have the last loop worked into the Y gap on the right-hand side. The subsequent row of loops will have the first loop on the left-hand side worked into gap Y, and the last loop worked into X. An alternative is to consistently work into the X half gaps on the left-hand side, and Y full gaps on the right-hand side. Under these circumstances the parallel edges will gradually slant to the left. The edges will slant to the right if the full gaps are worked on the left-hand side and the half gaps on the right-hand side.

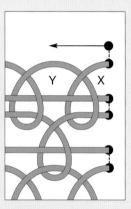

However, the most common form of shaping found on historic items was composed of loops worked into the same type of gap on both sides. As a result the motifs smoothly change size, increasing or decreasing by a single loop in each row. Another outcome of this gentle shaping is that the edge stitches are more uniform, enhancing the overall appearance of the motif. To gradually increase the stitching, use the half gaps marked X, and steadily move the entry/exit points outwards. To decrease, always work the loops into the full gaps marked Y, and gradually move the entry/exit points inwards.

It is possible to make more pronounced shaping. To increase the size of the stitching extend the position of the entry/exit points, and work some Elizabethan blanket stitches into the fabric as if one is starting a new row. For more dramatic decreases in the stitching area, simply turn before reaching the end of the previous row. Whilst this works well on the left-hand side, a sharp decrease on the right-hand side will expose the straight thread of the previous row. This can be avoided by extending the underneath section of the turn so that the straight line starts in the decreased position.

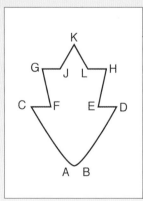

Historic motifs are often shaped in sympathy with the technique, such as this simplified leaf shape that is frequently seen of surviving items (for example, see Fig. 98, page 89 and Fig.156, page 147). The first row of blanket stitches is worked from A to B. Elizabethan corded detached buttonhole is used for the subsequent rows. The rows up to CD gradually increase by a single stitch each row (by working all the turns into half gaps X). At D the underneath section of the right-hand turn is extended so that the thread exits the fabric at E and works a right-to-left row to F. Subsequent rows gradually increase in size until row GH when another exaggerate decrease is made in the same manner as EF. The rows from LJ onwards gradually decreased by a single stitch each row (by working into full gaps Y) until the motif reaches a point and finishes at K.

120

'Bordered' turns

This type of turn produces a raised border edge to the stitching, and can be enhanced by making the gentle and consistent shaping described opposite. Here, the diagrams illustrate increasing edges on both sides as the first and last stitches of the row are made into X half gaps. The turns do have a tendency to curl inwards, though this is reduced when working at a fine scale .

Turning on the right-hand side

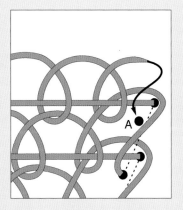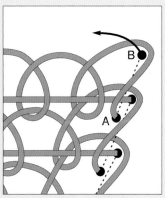

Bring the needle down to the right, going over two threads (the straight thread and the arms of the last loop in the previous row). Take the needle into the fabric at A, close to the previous exit point. Make sure the thread remains in an arch shape above the stitching. Bring the needle underneath the fabric from bottom-to-top, and exit at B, a short distance above the entry point. Make sure that the needle exits within the arch, before going over the thread at the top of the arch, ready to start the right-to-left stitching.

Turning on the left-hand side

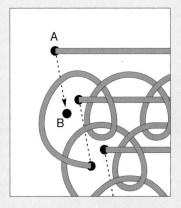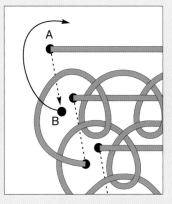

From A, bring the needle underneath the fabric, downwards and exit at B, a short distance from the previous entry point. Make sure that the needle exits within the arch made in the previous row. Bring the thread up over the top of this arch, and make a new arch above position A, before starting the left-to-right stitching.

Finishing

Finish on the right-hand side, and take the thread to the back of the fabric before securing it underneath. If you wish, you can make a couple of small couching stitches along the edge of the last row before securing the thread. However, many of the motifs found on historic examples were left with the last row loose from the fabric.

Elizabethan corded Brussels stitch

In keeping with modern practice, this book separates the embroidered Elizabethan corded detached buttonhole stitch from the needlelace version, Elizabethan corded Brussels stitch. Today, needlelace is supported during its production. All the edge stitches are taken around a border thread, known as a *cordonnet* or *foundation cord* (See Fig. 131). This is a separate thick thread that is temporarily couched down onto a flat surface. The cordonnet supports the needlelace during the working process, and afterwards, when the couching thread has been cut away from the flat surface, the cordonnet continues to support and border the finished stitching. These completed sections of needlelace can be couched down onto fabric to form what is known today as *raised* or *stumpwork*, a term that is often attributed to the work that became popular in the latter half of the 17th century.

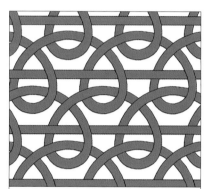

Fig. 130. Structure created by Elizabethan corded Brussels stitch.

However, the distinction between embroidery and needlelace seems less evident when examining earlier historic items. Examples of needlelace without a cordonnet were found, and there is evidence to suggest that these could be worked without a supporting surface, quite literally *punto in aria* (stitches in air). Today, this term is used to describe a particular type of needlelace (worked with a cordonnet on a supporting surface), yet early references to the word place it among embroidery stitches. Although the term's historic use is uncertain, this book will retain its association with embroidery, rather than needlelace. Therefore, the more literal interpretation of punto in aria will be used, as it bares more relevance to the techniques illustrated here. Structurally there is little difference between the punto in aria and embroidered versions except one exists in mid-air whilst the other pierces the fabric as the thread turns to work the next row. Indeed, Fig. 94 (page 83) illus-

trates how the embroidered stitch, with its edges worked into the fabric, simply lifts off the fabric and continues in the air.

Separate sections of Elizabethan corded Brussels stitch were usually found forming small petal shapes. These were individually attached onto a background fabric with a fine thread, and arranged so that they created three-dimensional flowers. As with many of the punto in aria examples, the motifs were often made with passing threads. The metallic content of the thread helps the petals to hold their shape, but it also helps support the stitching during its production. The first couple of rows are the most challenging, as there is little to grasp between the fingers. However, it gets easier as the work progresses and a comfortable rhythm is established. See Fig. 140 (page 128) for tips on how to work punto in aria.

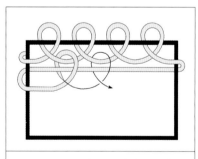

Fig. 131. Modern corded Brussels worked around a thick cordonnet thread.

An example of Elizabethan corded Brussels is illustrated in Case Study 12 (page 76) and 23 (page 148).

A start

The start is basically the same as that seen on page 119, except that the thread does not pierce any fabric. Fold the thread in half and position it so that the fold is on the right-hand side. It is easier to make the folded section a little longer than the required length, and draw up the surplus when the work is complete. Make a series of loops over the folded thread, starting on the left-hand side. There is a tendency for these stitches to twist around the folded thread. Don't worry - they can be flattened out later.

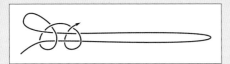

At the end of the row, when the desired number of loops has been made, take the needle between the two folded threads. Bring the needle back to the start, and take it through the leftmost gap, ready to begin working a normal row from left-to-right.

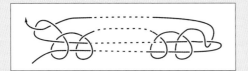

Shaping

As with the previous stitch, gentle shaping is controlled by deciding which gaps to use for the first and last loops. Here, the diagrams both show stitches working into the half X gaps, so that the motif gradually increases. To decrease use the full Y gaps.

Stitching from left-to-right

Step One:
Bring the needle down to the right, going over two threads (the straight thread and a rung). Take the needle into the gap between the loops.

Step Two:
Bring the needle up and under two threads (the same ones as in step one). Then bring the needle out over the working thread so that a new loop is formed.

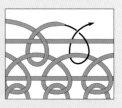

Turning on the right-hand side

No extra action is required.

Stitching from right-to-left

Step One:
Take the needle from right-to-left, and bring the needle through the left-most gap in the previous row. Make sure the needle comes in from behind the stitching so that it goes under, then over the first arm of the row.

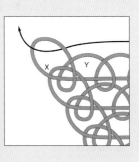

Turning on the left-hand side

No extra action is required.

Finishing

Finish on the right-hand side. Take the thread back through the previous stitching, either following a right-to-left straight line, or working around the outer edge.

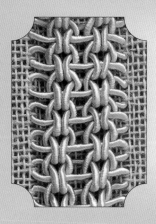

Elizabethan lark's head ladder stitch

A lark's head is one of the names given to the knot seen in Fig. 133. It is made of two loops, one with a Z-slanting crossover followed by a loop with an S-slanting crossover. These knots have been used in embroidery, such as in the *fancy buttonhole filling* seen in Fig. 134. Elizabethan lark's head ladder is different in that it has a straight line thread like the corded stitches shown on pages 118-122, though more significantly it varies because the lark's heads are connected into the knots rather than onto the rungs between the knots. As a result, the knots are arranged in vertical columns rather than staggered lines.

Although Elizabethan lark's head ladder stitch has similarities to Elizabethan Ladder stitch (page 110), it has been placed here because it belongs to the group of stitches made from *'loops connected over rungs',* rather than the Ceylon-style stitches made from *'loops connected around loops'.* However, it is worth noting a shared attribute. It was seen that the Ceylon-style stitches could be expanded from a single column of loops (page 106) to more than three columns of loops (page 114). Elizabethan lark's head ladder has two columns, each made from a pair of opposite-slanting loops. Nonetheless, this stitch can be expanded in the same way as the Ceylon-style stitches, and historic examples were found with different numbers of columns, as can be seen in Fig 135.

An example of Elizabethan lark's head ladder stitch is illustrated in Case Study 3 (page 49).

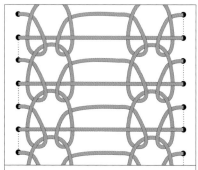

Fig. 132. Structure created by Elizabethan lark's head ladder.

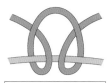

Fig. 133. A lark's head knot

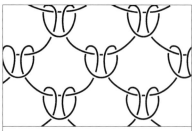

Fig. 134. Structure created by modern fancy buttonhole filling.

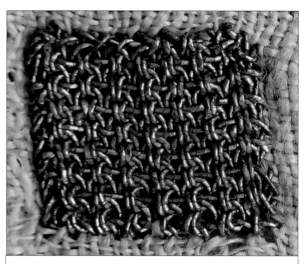

Fig. 135. An example of Elizabethan lark's head stitch with seven columns of knots rather than the two columns seen in Elizabethan lark's head ladder stitch. The sample block measures approximately 12 x 15mm and is found on Case Study 3.
© The Embroiderers' Guild

A start

Exit the fabric at position A, and take the needle over the surface, down to the right and enter the fabric at B. Take the needle up underneath the fabric, and exit at C. Make sure that the needle exits to the left of AB. Take the needle to the right and make a loose section over the surface before entering the fabric at D. Take the needle down underneath the fabric, and exit at E. Bring the needle up, underneath CD and over to the right. Repeat the same instructions on the right-hand side of the start. Enter the fabric at J, and take the needle up underneath the fabric to exit at K. Bring the needle from right-to-left and enter the fabric at L. Take the needle underneath the fabric from botton-to-top and exit at M, ready to start working normally.

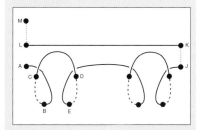

A finish

Finish after step four and secure the thread underneath the fabric.

Shaping

As with Elizabethan twisted chain (page 106).

Stitching bottom-to-top

Step One:
Surface section - Make a new loop into the gap between the two loops of the first lark's head. Do this by bringing the needle down over two threads (a straight line and a rung), then up underneath the same two threads before going over the working thread, from left-to-right.

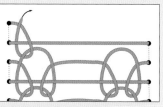

Step Two:
Surface section - Make another new loop into the same gap used in step one, but this time come in from behind. Do this by bringing the needle down under two threads (a straight line and a rung), then up over the same two threads, before going under the working thread, from left-to-right.

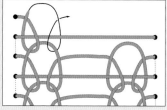

Step Three:
Surface section - Make a new loop into the gap between the two loops of the second lark's head. Do this by bringing the needle down over two threads (a straight line and a rung), then up underneath the same two threads before going over the working thread, from left-to-right.

Step Four:
Surface section - Make another new loop into the same gap used in step three, but this time come in from behind. Do this by bringing the needle down under two threads (a straight line and a rung), then up over the same two threads, before going under the working thread, from left-to-right. Enter the fabric just above the previous exit point.

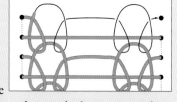

Step Five:
Underneath section - Bring the needle from bottom-to-top and exit the fabric a short distance above the entry point.

Step Six:
Surface section - Bring the needle from right-to-left and enter the fabric above the previous exit point.

Step Seven:
Underneath section - Bring the needle from bottom-to-top and exit the fabric a short distance above the entry point.

Elizabethan trellis stitch

The next two stitches are also constructed with loops, but here the connections differ as a new loop passes through, rather than behind, the previous loop. Elizabethan Trellis stitch is worked in rows, making Z-slant crossings when working from left-to-right and S-slant ones when working back from right-to-left. The alternate slants compact together to create a slightly raised hatched texture. The structure of modern trellis stitch is very different to the Elizabethan version, but the comparison is made because the modern stitch has been attributed to some of the historic examples. The modern stitch forms a series of half knots instead of loops, and these are worked over the rungs rather than through the previous loops. However, when the stitch is worked tightly, with the knots tilted, it bares a resemblance to the Elizabethan stitch.

Fig. 136. Structure created by Elizabethan trellis stitch

Historic examples were found worked in either silk or metallic passing, and as with other looped stitches they could be worked onto a background fabric or made punto in aria (see page 122). Here, the punto in aria version is explained, though it can easily be made into an embroidered version by working it over the surface of a fabric, and by taking the thread through the fabric as the stitching turns at the edge.

An example is illustrated in Case Study 21 (page 140) and Case Study 24 (page 149).

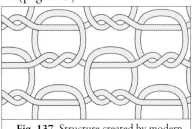

Fig. 137. Structure created by modern trellis stitch

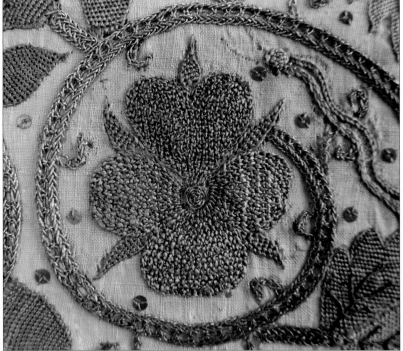

Fig. 138. Detail from Case Study 21 (page 140) showing a pansy motif worked in the embroidered version of Elizabethan trellis stitch. It measures less than 4 cm (1½ inches).
© *The Embroiderers' Guild.*

A start

As shown from Elizabethan corded Brussels (page 123)

A finish

Finish after step two, and take the thread back through the previous stitching to secure the end.

Shaping

Parallel edges are achieved by stitching the same number of loops in each row. This requires making the first stitch of the row into the last loop of the previous row. The diagram illustrates this for the right-hand turn.

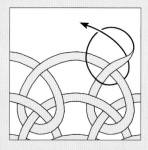

Working the first stitch of the row into the penultimate loop of the previous row will gradually decrease the edges of the stitching. Adding an extra loop onto the edge of the stitching will increase the size of the stitching. It is easier to add the new loop onto the outer rung, rather than add an extra loop into the last loop of the previous row.

Stitching from left-to-right

Step One:
Bring the needle to the right and down into the loop of the previous row. Note that it will pass over two threads (the crossover of the loop).

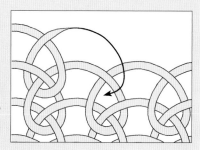

Step Two:
Bring the needle up to the right, making sure that it stays in front of the working thread, so that it creates a new loop. Note that the thread passes under two threads (the crossover of the loop) before it goes over the working thread. Continue repeating the two steps.

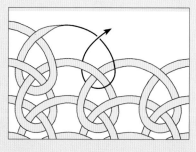

Turning on the right-hand side

No extra action is required for punto in aria, but if you are making the embroidered version, take the needle into the fabric, up underneath for a short distance and exit the fabric ready to continue stitching.

Stitching from right-to-left

Step One:
Bring the needle to the left and down into the loop of the previous row. Note that it will pass over two threads (the crossover of the loop).

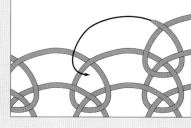

Step Two:
Bring the needle up to the left, making sure that it stays in front of the working thread, so that it makes a new loop. Note that the thread passes under two threads (the crossover of the loop) before it goes over the working thread. Continue repeating the two steps.

Turning on the left-hand side

No extra action is required for punto in aria, but if you are making the

Elizabethan corded trellis stitch (with two threads)

Elizabethan corded trellis stitch follows the same principle of Elizabethan corded detached buttonhole/Brussels in that the corded section of the stitch forms a straight line over which the loops are worked, though here the loops are taken into the loops of the previous row, rather than over the rungs. As with the previous stitches, Elizabethan corded trellis can be worked punto in aria, or embroidered by taking the thread into the fabric at the edge of the stitching. If the stitching is made with a single thread, it makes loops with Z-slanting crossovers on the left-to-right row and a straight line on the return row. The resulting structure is similar to Elizabethan corded detached buttonhole/Brussels in that all the loops cross over in the same direction. However, this example illustrates a version made from two separate threads, one creating the straight lines, the other making the looped stitches. Each thread zigzags back-and-forth in turn, and in the process the looped stitches form alternate rows of S- and Z-slanting crossovers.

Fig. 139. Structure created by Elizabethan corded trellis stitch with two

Here, the two thread version of Elizabethan corded trellis is shown working punto in aria. Only one needle is required, and it is used on the thread that is active making the loops. Although the straight-line thread is relatively passive, it is worth using passing for this section as the metallic thread has sufficient 'body' to support itself and the looped thread. It was effective for making vivid three-dimensional stitching, as the metallic passing can support a contrasting coloured silk thread. The same principle of working with two separate threads can also be applied to the Elizabethan corded detached buttonhole/Brussels stitches, such as seen on the walnut purse in the Victoria & Albert Museum (Accession Number T.57-1978).

An example of Elizabethan corded trellis is illustrated in Case Study 24 (page 149).

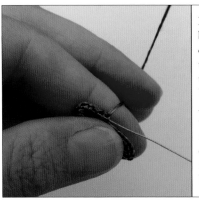

Fig. 140. *Punto in aria* is literally translated as 'stitches in air'. The term is used in this book to describe any stitching that is not supported on a fabric. Sections of punto in aria can be made in the hand as can be seen in the photograph. Here, the stitching is held in the left hand, between the thumb and index finger. The working thread is held under tension by taking it over the index finger and pinching it between the remaining fingers. Use the right hand to take the needle through the stitching, and draw up the slack thread. At the last moment, release the end of the working thread from the left hand. Draw up the remaining thread then pinch the working thread back between the left-hand fingers, ready to make the next stitch. This method can be applied to any punto in aria work. The example shown is being made with two threads: a straight-line thread of gilt passing that is firm enough to be self-supporting, and a working thread of green silk that is tensioned between the fingers.

A start

Pinch or knot the two threads together and keep this to the left-hand side. Take the needle and work a series of loops over the straight-line thread. There is a tendency for these stitches to twist around the folded thread. Don't worry - they can be flattened out later. When the desired number of loops has been made, you are ready to start working a normally with a turn on the right-hand side.

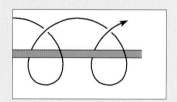

Finishing

Finish after step two, and take the thread back through the previous stitching to secure the end.

Shaping

The same as Elizabethan trellis stitch (page 127).

Stitching from left-to-right

Step One:
Lay the straight-line thread along the top of the previous row. Bring the needle to the right and down into the loop of the previous row. Note that it will pass over three threads (the straight line and the crossover of the loop).

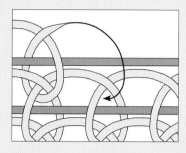

Step Two:
Bring the needle up to the right, making sure that it stays in front of the working thread, so that it creates a new loop. Note that the needle passes under three threads (the same ones passed over in step one), before going over the working thread.
Continue repeating the two steps.

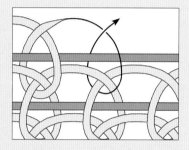

Turning on the right-hand side

Fold the straight-line thread up and to the left so that it lies along the top of the previous row.

Stitching from right-to-left

Step One:
Bring the needle to the left and down into the loop of the previous row. Note that it will pass over three threads (the straight line and crossover of the loop).

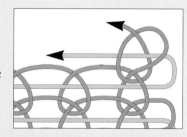

Step Two:
Bring the needle up to the left, making sure that it stays in front of the working thread, so that it makes a new loop. Note that the needle passes under three threads (the same ones passed over in step one), before going over the working thread.
Continue repeating the two steps.

Turning on the left-hand side

Fold the straight-line thread up and to the right so that it lies along the top of the previous row.

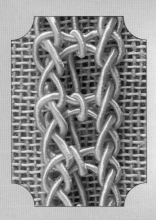

Elizabethan filling stitches

These filling stitches have been included here, not because they are looped stitches, but because they were usually found worked over the rungs of looped stitches, creating a composite stitch. The filling stitches were most often seen worked around the rungs of Elizabethan ladder stitch, though surviving examples were also found on other Ceylon-style stitches, and even on Elizabethan blanket stitch (see page 144).

As filling stitches were worked around the rungs of looped stitching, they remained above the surface of the fabric, though the start and the end of the thread were usually secured at the back of the fabric. The two parts of the composite stitching tended to be made with contrasting threads, typically a metallic passing for the underlying stitch, with a different passing or a silk thread for the filling. Many variations have been found, and just three are illustrated here. For each example you will need to make some initial Ceylon-style stitching. Here, is it assumed that Elizabethan ladder stitch has been worked. Remember to leave sufficient space between each stitch, so that there is room to add the filling.

Examples of Elizabethan filling stitches are illustrated in Case Study 3 (page 49), Case Study 21 (page 140) and Case Study 22 (page 144).

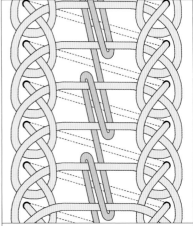

Fig. 141. The structure created by a filling of back stitches (under 4, back over 2) worked around the rungs of Elizabethan ladder stitch.

Back stitch filling

The most common type of filling found on examined items was a form of back stitch, though there was plenty of variation in the number of rungs that the thread passed over and under. The example illustrated takes the thread under four rungs and back over two, working so that an S-slant stitch is formed. If the filling stitches are firmly tensioned, it will draw together the pairs of rungs on the ladder stitch. The method is shown in the standard bottom-to-top manner, but the stitching is actually easier to work if the ladder stitch slants at an angle up to the left.

Back stitch variation

This variation of back stitch also goes back over two threads. However, it only travels underneath three rungs. As a consequence, the surface sections become staggered, so that two sections cover each rung. If the filling stitches are firmly tensioned the rungs of the ladder stitch will be drawn together to form a zigzag pattern.

Back stitch filling

A start

Bring the thread out of the fabric at the base of the ladder stitch, just below the centre of the first rung. Take the needle under the first two rungs of the ladder, ready to start working normally.

Stitching bottom-to-top

Step One:
Surface section - Bring the needle back down over two rungs, and to the right-hand side of the thread under the rungs.

Step Two:
Surface section - Take the needle upwards, going under four rungs of the ladder.
Continue repeating the two steps. Note that pulling firmly after step two will squeeze the pairs of rungs together.

A finish

Take the needle to the back of the fabric after step one has covered the last two rungs of the ladder. Secure the thread beneath the fabric under some of the previous stitching.

Shaping

Any shaping applied to the underlying stitch will automatically shape the filling as it follows the contours of the initial stitching.

Back stitch variation

A start

Bring the thread out of the fabric at the base of the ladder stitch, just below the centre of the first rung. Take the needle up under the first two rungs of the ladder, ready to start working normally.

Stitching bottom-to-top

Step One:
Surface section - Bring the needle back down to the left, over two rungs of the ladder.

Step Two:
Surface section - Take the needle up to the right, going under three rungs of the ladder.

Step Three:
Surface section - Bring the needle back down to the right over two rungs of the ladder.

Step Four:
Surface section - Take the needle up to the left, going under three rungs of the ladder.
Continue repeating the two steps.

A finish

Take the needle to the back of the fabric after step one has covered the last two rungs of the ladder. Secure the thread beneath the fabric under some of the previous stitching.

Shaping

Any shaping applied to the underlying stitch will automatically shape the filling as it follows the contours of the initial stitching.

Crochet chain

This more unusual filling is a form of chain stitch. Without the ladder rungs the structure would be known by a variety of names such as *crochet chain, monkey braid* or *trumpet cord*. The stitches are interlooped from a single thread, but as usual there is no conclusive evidence regarding its method of construction. Here, it is shown with the loops picked up from a thread that is taken 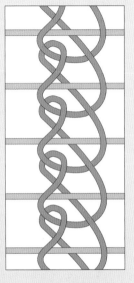 under the rungs of the ladder, but remain on the surface of the fabric. It will take up a large quantity of thread, so allow at least three times the required length, although you can always finish part way along the ladder, and restart with a new thread if necessary.

A finish

When you arrive at the last rung, take the needle up through the last loop. Bring the needle over the thread and enter the fabric to secure the last loop in place.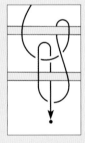

Shaping

Any shaping applied to the underlying stitch will automatically shape the filling as it follows the contours of the initial stitching.

A start

Bring the thread out of the fabric at the top of the ladder stitch, just above the centre of the first rung. Take the needle under all of the rungs of the ladder and leave it hanging at the bottom of the ladder. Use a small hook or the tip of a needle to lift a loop of the thread up over the first rung.

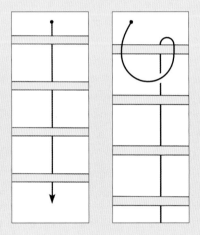

Stitching top-to-bottom

Surface section - Take the tip of the hook or needle into the loop resting over the rung, and pick up the thread lying under the rungs. Lift this thread so that it forms a new loop, and bring it towards you so that it rests over the next rung.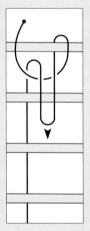

CASE STUDY 18

Example:
Elizabethan Blanket Stitch (page 100)
Object:
Pillow Bere
Location:
Witney Antiques, Oxfordshire

This large pillow bere, or pillow cover, measures approximately 55cm by 89cm (22 x 35inches). It is thought to date from the late 16th century. The plain-weave linen fabric has an embroidered border along two edges, and is covered with an all-over design of floral motifs surrounded by coiling stems. The repeated design is formed of three columns, each consisting of two different floral sprigs set within the coiling stems. The first column alternates between roses and pansies; the next column uses borage and carnations, whilst the third column has honeysuckle and cornflowers. Small birds and insects can also be found among the foliage. Although the design follows a repeated pattern, there are subtle variations, and the flowers are depicted in different colour arrangements. This interrupts the repetition, resulting in a varied and vibrant floral display.

It was not uncommon to find coiling stems bordered with small protruding stitches resembling thorns. For example, the clusters of three stitches seen on page 90. The pillow bere's coiling stems also exhibit

> **Fig. 142.** A large pillow bere with a design of coiling stems encircling floral motifs.
> © *Witney Antiques.*

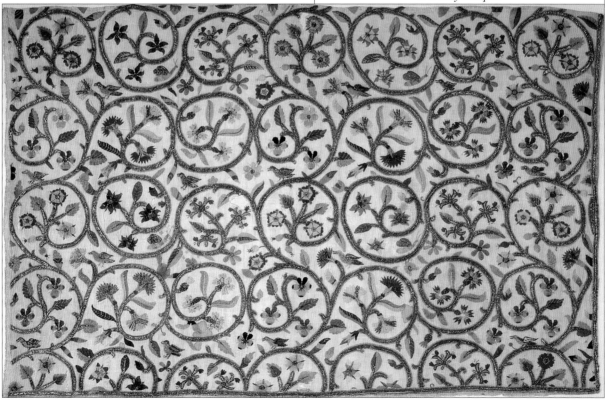

18

thorn-like spikes. The main stem of Elizabethan plaited braid stitch is worked in silver passing. It is bordered on both sides with Elizabethan blanket stitches. These stitches are worked in silk, using a subtle blend of different greens. The Elizabethan blanket stitches have been made with the top edge closest to the Elizabethan plaited braid stitch, so that the upper sections create a continuous green border-line to the stem. Meanwhile, each upright section extends away from the stem to produce the thorn-like elements.

Fig. 144. Close-up of the Elizabethan blanket stitches bordering the coiling stem.
© *Witney Antiques.*

Fig. 143. The front and back of the pillow bere
© *Witney Antiques.*

134

CASE STUDY 19

Example:
Elizabethan Double Looped Edging (page 104)
Object:
Coif
Location:
Private Collection

Fig. 145. The unfinished coif.
© *Privately owned. Copyright in the image reserved to the owner.*

This piece of fine plain-weave linen fabric has been marked with a blue ink or dye. The coloured lines depict a repeated coiling stem design that continues to the very edges of the fabric, and they have clearly seeped through to the back. The fabric measures roughly 27 cm by 46 cm (10½ x 18 inches), and within the confines of this area is a line of white running stitches that pick out the outline of a woman's coif. The shape is similar to those seen in Case Studies 13, 14 and 22, though this example remains unfinished. However, it does provide us with an insight into the stages of its production. All of the inked pattern within the coif's outline have been covered with coral stitch (see Fig. 113, page 104) worked in a dark

blue flossy silk. The lines of stitching are approximately 1mm wide, with an average of 9 stitches per centimetre (23 per inch). The only parts of the marked design that have not been covered are some of the small circles that sit within the curled leaf at the centre of every coiling stem.

In the middle of the coif is a block of coils that have not progressed beyond this initial stitching. Elsewhere, the embroiderer has enhanced the coral stitch with Elizabethan double looped edging, worked in a gilt passing thread. Most of these repeats also have their small circles covered, hidden under an

135

19

Fig. 147. The inked pattern has been covered in blue coral stitch. The outer repeats have been enhanced with the addition of Elizabethan double looped edging, worked in gilt passing. Some leaves have extra coral stitching used to portray the veins.
© *Privately owned. Copyright in the image reserved to the owner*

Elizabethan spider's web (see adjacent text). These are made from gilt metallic passing and are approximately 3mm in diameter. The 'spokes' are densely packed as the thread spirals around them approximately five times, resulting in the stitching sitting proud of the fabric in a small dome.

The intensity of the design has been amplified within some of the coils, by the addition of some more coral stitches. These have been used to insert fine vein-like blue lines into the curling leaves. One wonders how much of the total design was envisaged by the embroiderer before work commenced, or whether changes were decided upon as the appearance of the embroidery emerged. Certainly these leaf veins seem to have been an afterthought to the initial working of the coral stitches. A further sign of the

Fig. 146. A close-up of the curled leaf with the small circles covered in Elizabethan spider's webs.
© *Privately owned. Copyright in the image reserved to the owner*

Elizabethan spider's web

Exit the fabric at position A, and take the needle upwards and enter the fabric at B. Keep this surface stitch section loose, as the needle will need to pass underneath it several times. Bring the needle underneath the fabric down to the right and exit the fabric at C. Take the needle over the surface of the fabric from right-to-left, so that it makes a loose stitch section over AB and enters the fabric at D. Bring the needle underneath the fabric down to the right and exit the fabric at E.
The surface sections AB and CD meet at the centre X of the spider's web, and form four of the radial 'spokes'. The fifth spoke is made when the thread from E arrives at the centre X, ready to begin its clockwise journey spiralling outwards from the centre. The needle works a series of circular 'weaving' actions going alternately over and under the five spokes. Start with "over DX, under BX, over CX, under AX, over EX" and continue round with "under DX, etc", until the spokes are full. Here, the needle has been taken around the spokes five times and ends by going into the fabric at F.

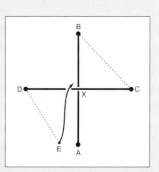

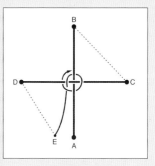

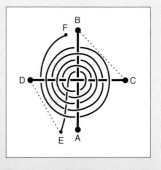

embroiderer's thinking progress can be seen in a little test piece on the edge of the fabric. Here, the coral stitches are worked in a paler blue silk than the main stitching. The test stitches are also a little denser, with around 11 stitches per cm (28 per inch). The addition of the gilt passing starts with an S-slanting version of Elizabethan looped edging, before switching to Elizabethan double looped edging.

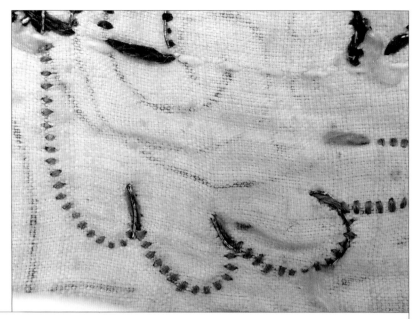

Fig. 148. The front and back of the test stitching at the edge of the fabric. Near the outline of white running stitches, the gilt passing is taken through the coral stitching in an S-slanting version of Elizabethan looped edging. After a short distance the embroiderer switches to Elizabethan double looped edging. Note the inked design has seeped through to the back of the fabric.
© Privately owned. Copyright in the image reserved to the owner

CASE STUDY 20

Example:
Elizabethan Twisted Chain (page 106)
Object:
Purse, or Sweet Bag
Location:
Gallery of Costume, Platt Hall, Manchester
Accession Number: 1948.4

This small purse measures just 11 cm high and 13 cm wide (4 x 5 inches), and is constructed in the same manner as the ones seen in Case Studies 7, 11 and 24. The background fabric is a plain weave linen with 14 threads per cm along a linear length (35 per inch). It is entirely covered in needlepoint depicting a trellis pattern. The spaces between the latticework are filled with alternating floral motifs, either a large five-petalled blue flower, or a pink bloom on a stalk. Despite the repeated geometric nature of the design, there is no evidence of systematic thread counting, as the size and layout of the design is inconsistent, and overall the work seems somewhat dense and haphazard. The lattice framework and the floral motifs have been executed in tent stitch using flossy silk threads. The erratic workmanship is visible in the motifs as some have the surface sections slanting in the same direction, whilst others have rows alternating between S- and Z-slant stitching. The same can be said of the background, which has been worked in Elizabethan reverse stitches using metallic passing. The stitches vary between S- and Z-slant, though their somewhat irregular arrangement means that they can hardly be referred to as Elizabethan knitting stitch. The intensity of the design is augmented with the addition of short sections of Elizabethan twisted chain stitch, worked in gilt passing. They have been used to fill the right-angled gaps in the framework, whilst Elizabethan spider's webs (page 136), cover the central squares.

Although the stitching is not particularly elegant, the scale of work is fine and the materials relatively costly. One could speculate that this is the product of an inexperienced embroiderer, or one becoming infirm, or even just a reluctant maker. Whatever the circumstance of its production, the purse has obvious signs of wear-and-tear suggesting that it served its function.

More information:
An image of thepurse is available on-line in the Gallery of Costume's "Search the collection" database.

Fig. 149. Sketch of the latticework pattern found on the sweet bag.

CASE STUDY 21

Example:
Elizabethan Double Ladder (page 112)
Elizabethan Filling Stitch (page 130)
Elizabethan Corded Detached Buttonhole (page 118)
Elizabethan Trellis Stitch (page 126)
Object:
Panel
Location:
Embroiderers' Guild Collection, London
Accession Number: EG 1982.79

Fig. 150. The panel of coiling stems encirlcing floral motifs.
© *Embroiderers' Guild*

This early 17th century panel is embroidered with an all-over design of coiling stems encircling floral motifs. The pattern is mirror-imaged about the central line and consists of four different columns each containing three coils. The two columns on the outer edges are only partially visible, and include an unidentified flower, thistle and foxglove. The next inner columns contain pea-pod, rose and pansy motifs. Columns of honeysuckle, cornflower and carnation follow these (the cornflowers are identified by the spaces between the petals). The single central column is an amalgam, with a repeat of one floral motif from each of the outer columns: thistle, pea-pod and cornflower, with a bird sitting between the latter two. The same arrangement of floral designs within coiling stems can be seen on a jacket held at the Victoria & Albert Museum (Accession number 1359-1900), though here there are three repeated columns each containing four motifs. The striking resemblance between the two artefacts provides strong evidence that the design was drawn from the same source.

The panel is made from plain-weave linen, with around 37-39 threads per linear centimetre (94-99 per inch), and measures 43 cm by 23 cm (17 x 9 inches). The embroidered design is framed with blue stem stitches, and the remains of a variation of Elizabethan blanket stitch can be seen along the top edge. Although some of the coiling stems are made of standard Elizabethan plaited braid stitch, most are Elizabethan double ladder with a filling of back stitch. The

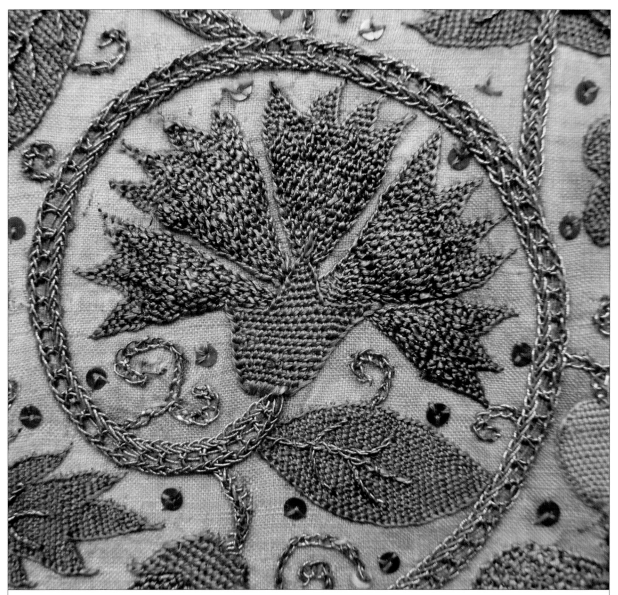

Fig. 151. A close-up detail of a cornflower motif. The green section has been made from Elizabethan corded detached buttonhole, with bordered turns, giving it a slightly raised edge. The same stitch has been used to make the outer tips of each petal. The rest of the petal has been worked in Elizabethan trellis stitch, using a silk wrapped in an elongated length of flat metal strip. The stitches are taken into the fabric at the turn of the rows. The petals are slightly raised as they have been worked over a small padded area at the centre of each petal. © *Embroiderers' Guild*

composite stitching has been worked in metallic passing and measures approximately 3 to 4mm in width with around 8 stitches per cm (20 per inch). In the bottom left-hand corner of the panel there is a small section of the Elizabethan double ladder where the filling thread has been taken twice around each pair of rungs (see Fig 152). It appears as if the embroiderer decided against this option because the rest is filled with a Z-slanting 'under 4, over 2' back stitch.

Most of the motifs incorporate Elizabethan corded detached buttonhole, with bordered turns, giving them a slightly raised edge. They are worked in a flossy silk, and different greens are often blended together to produce variegated tones for the leaves. The neat embroidery has around 13 to15 stitches per centimetre (33-38 per inch) and 11to 14 rows of

141

stitching per centimetre (28-35 per inch). In addition to the Elizabethan corded detached buttonhole, the large motifs have central sections worked in a silk that has been loosely wrapped with a thin flat strip of metal. This is used to make sections of Elizabethan trellis stitch. The stitch has been worked into the fabric at the edges, though a few sections transform into punto in aria so that they lift off from the surface (much like the Elizabethan corded detached buttonhole/Brussels seen in Fig. 94, page 83). The three-dimensional qualities have been enhanced with the addition of padding hidden between the fabric surface and the embroidery. The raised peapods are worked differently to the other motifs in that although the base layer is Elizabethan corded detached buttonhole, the upper section is formed from two threads: a gilt passing and a green silk. The stitching is not Elizabethan trellis stitch, but a variation of corded detached buttonhole (see adjacent text). At the start of this stitching, the green silk is worked over the passing and into the fabric. As it continues, the threads turn into the fabric at the edge nearest the stalk, whilst at the other edge they turn punto in aria. The final row of stitching is also left unattached, creating two free edges. Once again, there is no evidence of a cordonnet. The peapods measure about 3cm by 1cm wide, with around 9 stitches per cm (23 per inch).

Fig. 152. Detail of Elizabethan double ladder worked in metallic passing. The right-hand section has been filled with a single passing thread that has been taken twice around each pair of rungs. However, the majority of the coiling stems are filled with the Z-slanting 'under 4, over 2' back stitch, as seen in the left-hand section.
© Embroiderers' Guild

Peapod stitch

The structure of the peapod stitching is a variation of corded detached buttonhole that has similarities to modern *lace filling* stitch. The historic example is made from a passing thread that works back-and-forth creating the corded straight-line 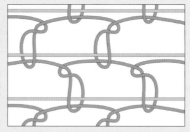 part of the stitching. A separate green silk thread has been worked over each line, making a form of buttonhole stitch with an extra turn at the head of the loop. As this thread travels back-and-forth, the crossovers alternate between S- and Z-slanting.

Fig. 153 (Opposite). A stalk, made of standard Elizabethan plaited braid stitch, supports a peapod filled with peas, made from Elizabethan spider's webs (similar to those seen on page 136). The peapod's base is Elizabethan corded detached buttonhole stitch, and the upper section is worked in a type of *lace filling* stitch (see above). The stitching at the start and the edge nearest the stalk are taken into the fabric whilst the other edges are worked punto in aria. The outer loose edge consists of the final row that is worked from the stalk downwards, and remains unattached. The last row then continues down over the loose side of the stitching (where the threads have turned to start new rows during the pod-making), until the passing and green silk arrive at the end of the starting edge where they are taken to the back of the fabric and secured.
© Embroiderers' Guild

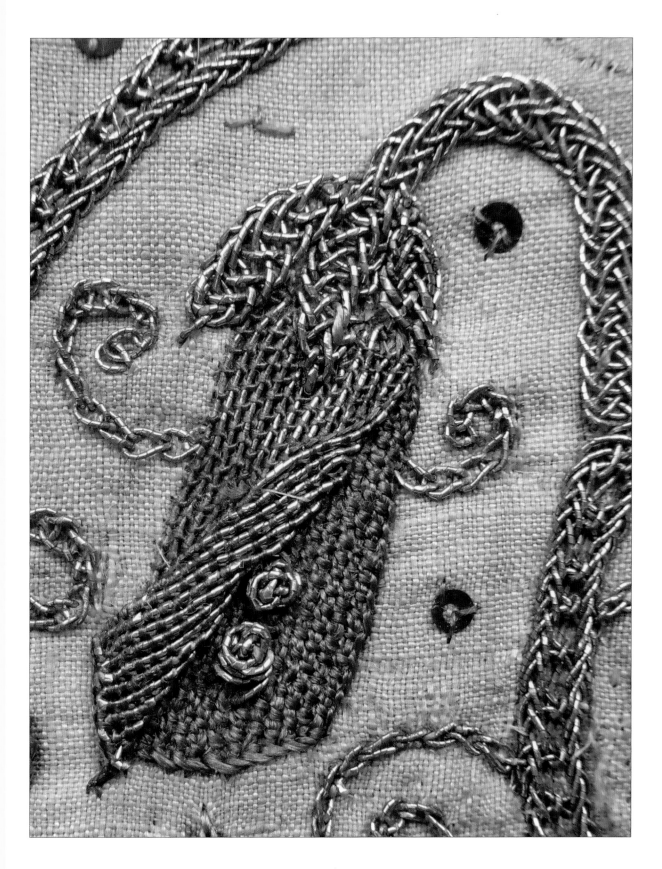

CASE STUDY 22

Example:
Elizabethan Corded Detached Buttonhole (page 118)
Elizabethan Blanket Stitch (page 100)
Elizabethan Filling Stitch (page 130)
Elizabethan Plaited Braid Stitch-Variation One (page 70)
Object:
Coif
Location:
Witney Antiques, Oxfordshire

This coif is said to date from around 1600, and is made for a single piece of linen that has been cut to shape like those seen in previous Case Studies 13, 14 and 19. The fine plain-weave linen measures approximately 24 cm (9 inch) in height and between 31 and 42 cm (12-16 inches) in width. The bottom edge of the linen has been folded over to make a hollow hem, through which is threaded a tie made from a tiny woven band. The other edges have been hemmed and decorated with a variation of Elizabethan blanket stitch, and the top seam has been gathered at the crown of the head.

The embroidered design is conventional as it consists of coiling stems encircling floral motifs. However, each stem supports an unusual combination of stylised flowers, fruit and insects. The same design, worked in the same stitches, has been found on a forehead cloth in the Victoria & Albert Museum (Accession Number T76-1911). Although there is debate about how this triangular piece of fabric was worn, documentary evidence and surviving examples reveal that forehead cloths and coifs were made as matching sets.

Fig. 154. Close-up of the coif seen on the opposite page. The main stems are Elizabethan plaited braid stitch (variation one), and the slightly thinner stems are Elizabethan blanket stitch, with a crochet chain filling.
© Witney Antiques

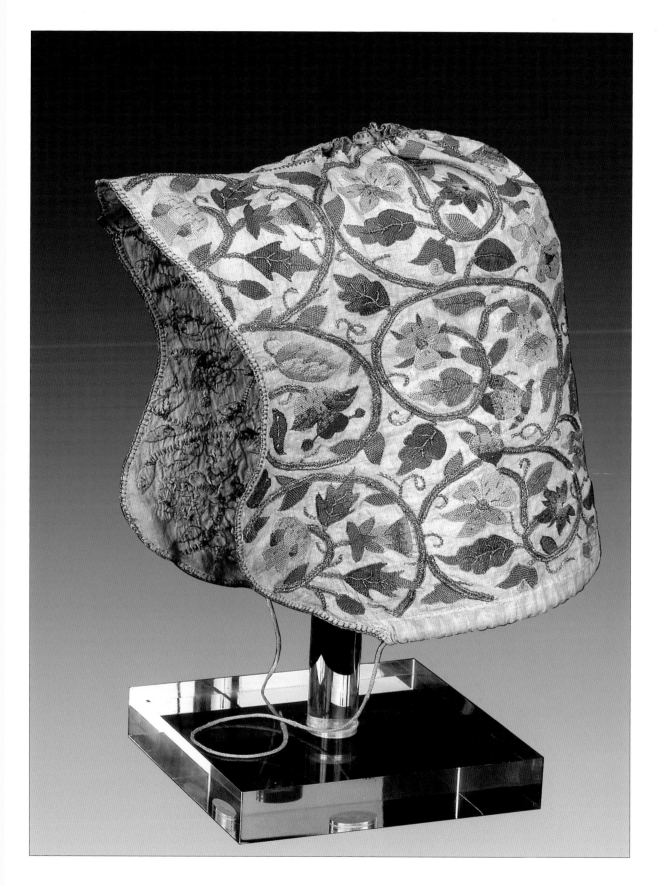

The coiling stems are embroidered using metallic passing thread. The main stems are approximately 3 mm wide, and worked in Elizabethan plaited braid stitch (variation one), with around 8 stitches per centimetre (20 per inch). The slightly thinner stems are around 2 mm wide, and also have around 8 stitches per centimetre (20 per inch), but they are worked in Elizabethan blanket stitch. The same passing thread has been used to add a crochet chain filling onto the underlying stitches, to help give them a little more volume. The stems reach out to motifs that have been worked in coloured silks using Elizabethan corded detached buttonhole stitch with bordered turns. Most of the motifs are gently shaped so that the stitching increases or decreases by a single stitch every row. This gives rise to the distinctive stylised forms of the motifs, and enhances the bordered turns so that they create a noticeable raised ridge around the outer edge of the motif. On some of the motifs, extra chain stitches have been used to finish the tips in elegant extended points (see opposite page). The embroidery is fine with around 17 stitches along a centimetre length (43 per inch) and 14 rows of stitching per centimetre (35 per inch).

Fig. 155. Front and back of a hip motif. It measures around one centimetre in height.
The red silk is worked in Elizabethan corded detached buttonhole with bordered turns.
The gentle increasing and decreasing of the bordered turns creates a distinctive raised ridge that frames the motif.
© Witney Antiques

Leave tips

An illustration of a chain stitch added at the end of a row of Elizabethan corded detached buttonhole. This can be used to extend a leaf-tip before making a more pronounced decrease and continuing with another leaf-tip.

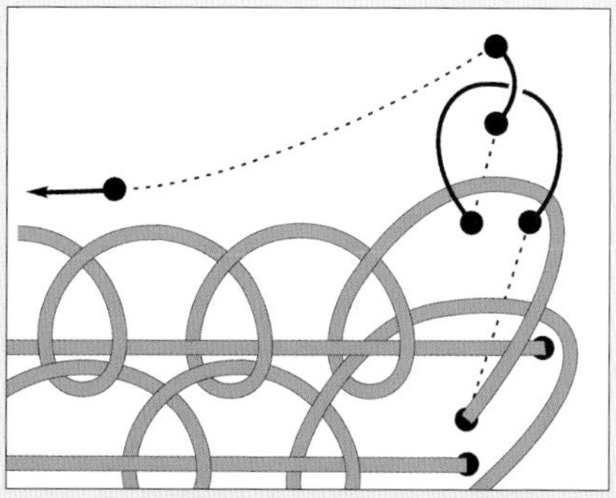

Fig. 156. A typical leaf shape worked in Elizabethan corded detached buttonhole with bordered turns. As the stitching reached the leaf-tips, chain stitches were used to extend the points.

© Witney Antiques

147

CASE STUDY 23

Example:
Elizabethan Corded Brussels (page 122)
Applied Work (page 152, 153 & 156)
Object:
Book Cover
Location:
British Library, London
Shelfmark:
C.65.k.5.(1.)

Robert Barker and John Bill (page 60) also printed this copy of *The Holy Bible* in 1642. It is fairly small, measuring approximately 15 cm high and 8½ cm wide (6 x 3 inches), with a spine width of 3½ cm (1 inch). Handwritten on the first page is the name 'Mary Bacon' though there is no date to establish if she was the original owner.

At first glance the book appears to have a pink silk satin cover that has been decorated with metallic threads. However, the fabric is just a thin strip of fabric, cut on the bias, and pasted down over the rim of the book cover. The applied decoration has been worked onto vellum or parchment. The background consists of a bundle of twelve strands of metallic passing that zigzags over the cover, from the top to bottom edges. The bundle has been couched down in long and rather uneven stitches worked in white silk. Further embroidery helps to secure the bundle in place. Couched down passing threads have also been used to create the sculptural oval frame that dominates the stylised design. It is surrounded by motifs that are outlined with couched down cords. These are Z-twisted 2-ply, with each ply consisting of a single passing thread. The cords border areas filled with various fancy threads that have been couched down onto the background with a separate thread, and include short sections of purl laid parallel to one another.

At the centre of the oval is a padded circle surrounded by four petal-shapes. As with the other motifs, these are bordered with twisted cords. The red tips of the petals result from couching down a fancy cord. It is a loosely Z-twisted 2-ply cord, with one ply consisting of red silk and the other an elongated coil of round wire. Finally, these plied materials have been S-wrapped with an elongated strip of flat metal. The red petal tips

are partially covered with a piece of Elizabethan corded Brussels. Each tiny section has been worked in metallic passing, and measures approximately 1½ cm in height and 2cm at its widest. The punto in aria stitching has been attached down afterwards, over the top of a small area of padding. Just the base and two sides of the petal shape are secured, leaving the four tips free to add to the three-dimensional effect. The petal's shaping plays to the strengths of the technique, as each row gradually increases by a single stitch, before the end neatly divides and narrows into four pointed tips.

More information:
An image of the book cover is available on-line in the British Library's database of bookbindings.

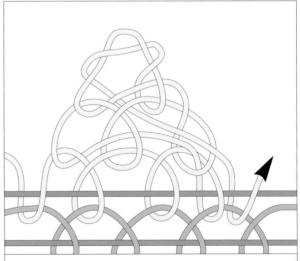

Fig. 157. A diagram illustrating the path of the thread making a petal tip.

CASE STUDY 24

Example:
Elizabethan Ground Stitch (page 28)
Elizabethan Trellis and Corded Trellis (page 126 & 128)
Elizabethan Tubular Ceylon (page 116)
Applied Work (page 157)
Object:
Purse, or Sweet bag
Location:
Salisbury & South Wiltshire Museum, Salisbury
Accession Number: 1929.5

This small purse or sweet bag is lavishly embroidered with metallic threads and silk. Today, the metal has tarnished and the silk faded, but in its original condition it would have made an impressive impact, and would have represented a costly investment. The bag measures around 10 cm square (4 inches) and is made of plain-weave linen with around 14 threads per linear centimetre (35 per inch). A design of coiling stems encircling floral motifs fills both of sides of the purse, and the background is completely covered with Elizabethan ground stitch worked in metallic passing, though the top edge changes to pink silk. Although most of the stitches cover the surface in (1:4) sized sections, some are altered to help the stitching to fit around the contours of the design.

The five main motifs are a carnation, grapes, cornflower, borage and rose. They have been built up from a base of silk tent stitch. The petals, made using Elizabethan trellis and corded trellis stitch, were worked separately and attached after completion. As they have only been partially couched down, the tips of the petals lift up creating a three-dimensional effect. The petals were made with a variegated passing, consisting of a silk core wrapped in a flat strip of metal that has been slightly elongated so that some of the coloured silk is visible. Other motifs depicting caterpillars and butterflies can also be found among the flowers. Their bodies measure around 5mm wide, and they have been made using Elizabethan tubular Ceylon stitch, with around 9 stitches per centimetre (23 per inch). They have also been made separately and couched down onto the bag afterwards. All the motifs have been further embellished with spangles and various thicknesses of purl made from strips of flatten metal.

Fig. 158. This small purse is typical of the type referred to as a sweet bag. It is made from a rectangle of linen fabric folded along the base and seamed at the sides. The bag has two braid drawstrings that terminate in ornate tassels, and a matching braid handle. Three small tassels adorn the base, and a further two features sit within the top two corners. The bag's suface is richly decorated in three-dimensional embroidery.
© Courtesy of Salisbury & South Wiltshire Museum.

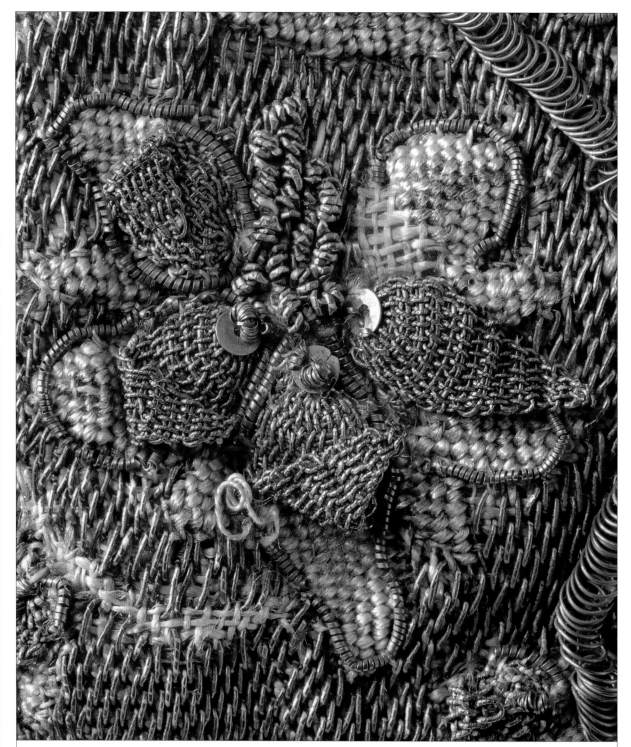

Fig. 159. Detail of the borage motif made from sections of Elizabethan corded trellis that have been partially couched down to produce the three-dimensional petals. One petal is missing, revealing the extent of the silk tent stitch base and the plain-weave linen fabric. Note also the spangles held in place with a small circle of purl at their centre.
© Courtesy of Salisbury & South Wiltshire Museum.

Applied Work

The next section looks at ornamentation created by applying decorative features onto a fabric. Sometimes the applied ornamentation provided a highlighted detail, and was used in conjunction with other needlework techniques. In other cases, the applied work depicted the main design, notably metallic arabesque patterns on silk satin or velvet. Typically, the surviving examples of applied work consisted of metal items couched down onto the fabric's surface. This emphasized the visibility to the metal, and was an effective use of these costly components. However, other materials, such as pearls and glass beads were also applied to produce decorative effects.

All of these components were applied using a technique referred to as *couching*. This entails attaching the ornamentation by working a separate thread from underneath the fabric, over the ornamentation and back underneath the fabric. At times, the couching stitches were discrete, and either blended into the background or were hidden from view. On other occasions, they added to the effect by creating a well-defined pattern, or providing a contrasting colour. Generally, only the surface sections of the couching stitches are of importance, whilst the path of the underneath sections can be adapted to suit.

Passing

Metallic passing was not just used for embroidery stitches, but was found couched down onto fabric. It was used to make fine details, such as veins on a leaf or simple borders around motifs. It was also used more substantially to cover the fabric by travelling back and forth over an area, either as a single thread or as a small bundle of several threads. Sometimes the passing entered and exited the fabric as the thread turned at the edges. On other occasions, it remained on the surface and was secured at each turn with a small couching stitch. Further couching stitches and additional features could be worked over the top to help keep these areas of passing in place. This method had the potential of being relatively economic, in both time and materials. Couched bundles could cover large areas of fabric quicker and easier than other needlework techniques, and most of the costly metallic thread remained visible on the surface. Passing was also couched down into more impressive sculptural designs, by using padded sections and well defined couching stitches.

Example of applied passing are illustrated in Case Study 2 (page 48), Case Study 4 (page 52) and Case Study 23 (page 148).

A start

Secure the passing and couching thread underneath the fabric and bring the passing thread through to the surface of the fabric.

Couching

Step One:
Lay the passing along the line you wish to cover. Take the couching thread a short distance underneath the fabric, and exit the fabric so that the needle is alongside the passing.

Step Two:
Take the needle over the top of the passing and enter the fabric on the other side, so that a small stitch section is formed perpendicular to the passing.

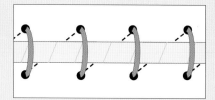

A finish

Take the end of the passing to the back of the fabric, and secure both threads underneath.

Shaping

The passing can be curved in any direction to create outlines and shapes, or it can be zigzagged back-and-forth to fill an area.

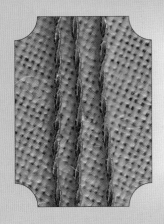

Twisted cords

Twisted cords were used in a similar way to passing, though they were thicker and created more prominent features. They were flexible enough to be couched down in complex shapes and curves. As a consequence they were used extensively for motif borders and for the arabesque designs that were popular throughout the 16th to 17th century. The cords were usually 2-ply, made from twisting together two metallic passing threads. However, many other combinations were found, providing a wide range of visual effects. Even a subtle change in the twist direction was put to good use, as the careful arrangement of S- and Z-twist cords lying side-by-side can mimic the appearance of a more complex braid.

The couching stitches tended to be hidden from view. They either went over the top of the cord following the angle of the ply, so that they sat within the grove, or they just went over one of the cord's plies. The exit and entry holes are usually positioned closer together than shown in the diagram, so that they sit slightly underneath the cord and are hidden from view.

Examples of applied twisted cords are illustrated in Case Study 2 (page 48) and Case Study 23 (page 148).

A start

Secure the couching thread underneath the fabric. Where possible secure the cord underneath the fabric and bring it through to the surface of the fabric. If the cord is too thick, fold the end underneath itself and secure with a couple of couching stitches.

Couching

Step One:
Lay the cord along the line you wish to cover. Take the couching thread a short distance underneath the fabric, and exit the fabric so that the needle is alongside the cord, close to the groove between two plies.

Step Two:
Bring the needle over the top of the cord. Follow the angle of the groove, and enter the fabric on the other side, so that the surface stitch section sits within the groove.

A finish

Take the end of the cord to the back of the fabric, and secure both threads underneath. Alternatively, tuck the end of the cord underneath itself and secure with a couple of couching stitches.

Shaping

The cord can be curved in any direction to create outlines and shapes, or it can be zigzagged back-and-forth to fill an area.

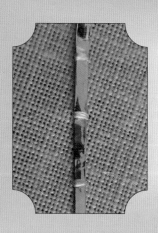

Plate

Thin strips of metal sheet, referred to as *plate*, were found couched down onto fabric, providing a solid line of reflective ornamentation. The strips typically measure around 2 or 3 mm wide. Although the metal is pliable, there are limits to its capability. In spite of this, different effects were achieved by making small folds in the strip. Two examples are shown here.

An example of applied plate is illustrated in Case Study 6 (page 55).

Fig. 160. Detail of the panel in Case Study 6 (page 55). The sun motif is made from strips of corrugated plate and lines of twisted cords.
© *Ashmolean Museum, University of Oxford.*

A start

Lay the strip of metal onto the fabric's surface, but pointing away from the direction you wish cover. Bring the needle out of the fabric at A, close to the start of the strip. Take the needle over the strip and enter the fabric at B. Lift the end of the strip up and over the thread, so that the start of the strip is hidden underneath itself. Push down firmly on the end of the strip, so that the metal is well folded.

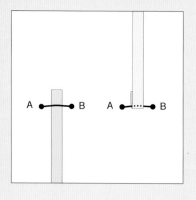

A finish

Fold the end of the strip over the top of the last couching stitch.

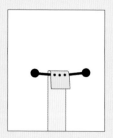

Flat and corrugated lines

Small sections of flat plate were couched down, though the rigidity of the metal meant it could only be used in straight lines, However, a corrugated strip was a little more flexible, and allowed the metal to be couched down in gentle curves. A corrugated strip has small dents in the metal, creating troughs and peaks. The dents lie perpendicular to the edges, so that they produce little waves undulating along the strip.

Couching

Step One:
Take the needle underneath the fabric, and exit at A, close to the edge of the strip. If you are working with a corrugated strip, this will be at the next trough.

Step Two:
Take the needle over the metal strip, and enter the fabric at B, close to the opposite edge of the strip. When using a corrugated strip, the thread will lie in the trough of the strip.

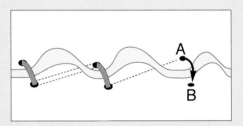

Shaping

A small amount of curvature can be added to the corrugated strips by gradually taking the exit/entry points further to the left or right.

Zigzagged areas

Flat strips of plate were also found filling in small areas of a design, such as floral petals and leaves. Here, the strip is folded back over itself so that the reverse side is visible. The fold lines are at a slight angle to the perpendicular so that the strip does not completely cover itself, but zigzag back and forth over an area.

Couching

Step One:
Bring the needle underneath the fabric and exit at A, on the lower edge of the outline where you want the strip to fold.

Step Two:
Bring the needle up and over the strip, and enter the fabric at B.

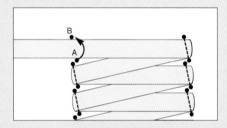

Step Three:
Fold the strip over the top of the stitch section AB at a slight angle, so that it zigzags back to the other side of the motif.
Continue repeat the three steps on each side of the motif.

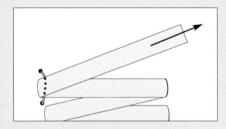

Shaping

Altering the angle and the distance between each fold can shape the areas being covered.

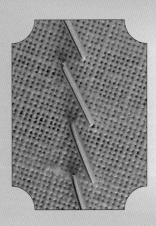

Purl

Purl was used in a variety of ways, and the range of sizes and shapes helped to add to the pattern potential. Coils of round wire produce a different texture to coils of flattened metal, and some designs took advantage of this attribute by carefully alternating the types. Small sections of purl were couched down to make highlight 'spots', or arranged in groups to create textured areas, and longer lengths were used to outline borders. The couching thread was usually taken through the central hollow of a short section of purl, but longer pieces were often attached in a similar fashion to twisted cords, with couching threads taken over at an angle between the coils. The spots of purl can appear as long 'dashes' if the surface section of the couching stitch is the same length as the purl, and the needle exits and enters the fabric just beyond the ends of the purl. Alternatively, the exit and entry points can be placed closer together. This forces the centre of the purl up off the fabric to create a raised spot. If the exit and enter points of the couching thread are in the same place, then a little raised circle of purl is formed like the version illustrated on page 157. The example illustrated here was used to create fillings for motifs, with the parallel sections of purl forming a ribbed texture.

An example of applied purl is illustrated in Case Study 4 (page 52) and Case Study 23 (page 148).

A start

Secure the couching thread underneath the fabric, and exit the fabric at the start of the motif.

A finish

Secure the couching thread underneath the fabric.

Couching

Step One:

Cut the purl to the required length (here, the width of the motif). Take the needle through the central hollow of the coil, and enter the fabric at the end of the purl. Note that the stitch section is the same length as the purl, so that it lies flat on the fabric.

Step Two:

Take the needle a short distance underneath the fabric, and exit just above the entry point. Continue repeating the two steps keeping the purl sections parallel to one another.

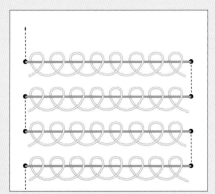

Shaping

Varying the length of purl can shape the motifs. Continue to lay the purl in parallel lines, but alter the exit and entry points to accommodate the changes in length.

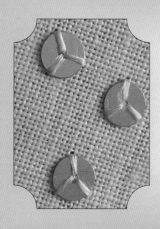

Spangles

Spangles were used as a highlight anywhere within a design. Sometimes they were used as just am occasional embellishment, whilst other historic examples were found with their backgrounds liberally dotted with spangles (for example, see Case Study 12, page 76). Other items exhibited evidence that spangles had once adorned them, but the actual metal had since been removed, either intentionally or by wear and tear. Today, sequins form a complete ring, but historic spangles were cut out by hand and have a small slit in them. As a consequence it is best to use two or three stitches over the ring to prevent the spangle from slipping free. Alternatively, a small section of purl can be used to secure the spangle. Here, the purl is attached as a raised spot, with both the exit and entry point sitting within the inner hole of the spangle.

An example of applied spangles is illustrated in Case Study 24 (page 149).

A start

Secure the couching thread underneath the fabric, and exit the fabric where you want the spangle to sit.

Couching

Step One:
Bring the needle through the central hole of a spangle, and through a short length of purl.

Step Two:
Bring the needle back down through the central hole of the spangle and enter the fabric.

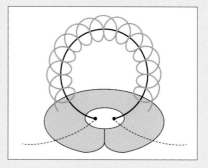

A finish

Secure the couching thread underneath the fabric.

Addresses

Arbury Hall
Arbury Park, Nuneaton, Warwickshire, CV10 7PT.
www.arburyestate.co.uk

Ashmolean Museum of Art & Archeology
Beaumont Street, Oxford, OX1 2 PH
www.ashmolean.org

Bodleian Library
Broad Street, Oxford, OX1 3BG
www.bodleian.ox.ac.uk

British Library
St Pancras, 96 Euston Road, London, NW1 2DB
www.bl.uk

Burrell Collection
2060 Pollokshaws Road, Glasgow, G43 1AT
www.glasgowmuseums.com

Dorset County Museum
High West Street, Dorchester, Dorset, DT1 1XA
www.dorsetcountymuseum.org

Embroiderers' Guild
1 Kings Road, Walton on Thames, Surrey, KT12 2RA
www.embroiderersguild.com

Platt Hall (The Gallery of Costume)
Rusholme, Manchester, M14 5LL
www.manchestergalleries.org

Salisbury & South Wiltshire Museum
65 The Close, Salisbury, SP1 2EN
www.salisburymuseum.org.uk

Victoria & Albert Museum
Cromwell Road, London, SW7 2RL
www.vam.ac.uk

Witney Antiques
96-100 Corn Street, Witney, Oxfordshire, OX28 6BU
www.witneyantiques.com

Supplies for the samples seen in this book came from:

Devere Silk
Weavers House, Hyde Wood Road, Little Yeldham,
Halstead, Essex, CO9 4QX
www.devereyarns.co.uk

Benton & Johnson Metallic threads
Regalia House, Newtown Road, Bedworth,
Warwickshire, CV12 8QR
www.bentonandjohnson.com

Golden Threads
Brimstone Cottage, Poundsley, Blackboys, East Sussex,
TN22 5HS
www.goldenthreads.co.uk

Angus Weavers
House of Dun, Montrose, Angus, DD10 9LQ

Zweigart Linen
www.zweigart.de

Books available from:
Carey Company
Summercourt, Ridgeway, Ottery St Mary, Devon,
EX11 1DT

Index